The **NO-NONSENSE GUIDE** to

GLOBALIZATION

'Publishers have created lists of short books that discuss the questions that your average [electoral] candidate will only ever touch if armed with a slogan and a soundbite. Together [such books] hint at a resurgence of the grand educational tradition... Closest to the hot headline issues are *The No-Nonsense Guides*. These target those topics that a large army of voters care about, but that politicos evade. Arguments, figures and documents combine to prove that good journalism is far too important to be left to (most) journalists.'

Boyd Tonkin,
The Independent,
London

About the author
Wayne Ellwood is a co-editor of the *New Internationalist* magazine.
www.newint.org

Other titles in the series
The No-Nonsense Guide to Fair Trade
The No-Nonsense Guide to Climate Change
The No-Nonsense Guide to World History
The No-Nonsense Guide to Science
The No-Nonsense Guide to Conflict and Peace
The No-Nonsense Guide to Human Rights
The No-Nonsense Guide to Animal Rights

About the New Internationalist
The **New Internationalist** is an independent not-for-profit publishing co-operative. Our mission is to report on issues of global justice. We publish informative current affairs and popular reference titles, complemented by world food, photography and gift books as well as calendars, diaries, maps and posters – all with a global justice world view.

If you like this *No-Nonsense Guide* you'll also love the **New Internationalist** magazine. Each month it takes a different subject such as *Trade Justice*, *Nuclear Power* or *Iraq*, exploring and explaining the issues in a concise way; the magazine is full of photos, charts and graphs as well as music, film and book reviews, country profiles, interviews and news.

To find out more about the **New Internationalist**, visit our website at
www.newint.org

The NO-NONSENSE GUIDE to
GLOBALIZATION

Wayne Ellwood

The No-Nonsense Guide to Globalization
First published in the UK by
New Internationalist™ Publications Ltd
Oxford OX4 1BW, UK
www.newint.org
New Internationalist is a registered trade mark.

Cover image: Wal-Mart in China. Wang Jun/Phototex/Camera Press.

Series editor: Troth Wells
Design by New Internationalist Publications Ltd.

 Printed on recycled paper by T J Press International, Cornwall, UK
who hold environmental accreditation ISO 14001.

British Library Cataloguing-in-Publication Data.
A catalogue record for this book is available from the British Library.

Library of Congress Cataloguing-in-Publication Data.
A catalogue for this book is available from the Library of Congress.

ISBN 10: 1-904456-44-8
ISBN 13: 978-1904456-445

Foreword

THIS IS AN important work for anyone concerned about the future of planetary life. It is a clear and richly factual overview of the global corporate system – from its colonial past beginning with Cristóbal Colón's famous 1492 search for a sea route to the fabled riches of East Asia, to the current regime of 'globalization' in which a comprehensive plan to subordinate domestic economies everywhere to transnational banking and corporate rule is now into high gear.

Ceaseless repetition of slogans of 'inevitable change' and 'necessary restructuring' have everywhere accompanied this rapid prying-open of national economies and cultures for foreign exploitation 'free of trade and investment barriers'. But there is an astonishing gap between the dominant ideology of a 'self-regulating global free market' and the reality of tens of thousands of trade-lawyer constructed regulations imposed across the world by a fast-moving, secretive process instituting the private demands of transnational corporations as absolute rights to which elected legislatures everywhere are made subordinate.

The fact is that the very opposite of a 'free market' is at work. Since the fall of the Berlin Wall, corporate financial interests and their mass media vehicles have together stormed governments with an overwhelming agenda for world corporate rule. The rules are political, but unspoken. Either governments competitively enact this agenda, or deregulated capital and election funding will go elsewhere and resistant leaders will be ignored or pilloried in the corporate press.

The public is reassured that 'a rising tide of growth will lift all boats'. The demand is that 'global market competition be made free of the tax and regulatory burdens of government'. But the harsh reality is the very opposite of rising standards of living and new freedoms for the world's peoples. On almost every indicator of social and ecological life – from health protection, literacy development and future vocations for the young to maintenance of biodiversity and the planet's security of air, water, soil and climate – the restructuring of societies for corporate globalization has been increasingly life-destructive.

This book's wide-lensed and well-informed coverage of the system's global operations exposes the life-blind economics at work in a graphic explanation of what is really going on. If there is to be a turning of global governance towards true sustainability, we need to recognize that it has to be in a direction that makes civil and planetary life sovereign instead of instrumentalizing both for the money-to-more-money feeding cycle of transnational financial interests.

This policy itself, in turn, can only be achieved by people awakening in large numbers to the spectacularly failed program of corporate globalization. *The No-Nonsense Guide to Globalization* provides a lucid explanatory map of our current condition. For all who seek to think past corporate slogans to life-responsible government, this is a concise and valuable overview of the world system, what has gone wrong with it – and the way ahead.

Professor John McMurtry,
Department of Philosophy,
University of Guelph,
Ontario, Canada.

CONTENTS

Introduction

WHEN THE FIRST edition of this book was published I described globalization as 'the most talked-about and perhaps the least understood concept of the new millennium'.

In the half-dozen years that have passed since those words were written the world has changed irrevocably. Globalization has entered the mainstream. And the fallout is everywhere.

The criminal and barbaric attacks of September 11, 2001 underlined, with murderous irony, the increasing contradictions of a globalizing world. As national and regional economies become more entwined, the idea of a global community with shared values and goals appears to be fading. In its place has emerged a determined attempt by the US to flout both domestic and international law as it wages a unilateral 'war on terror'.

The single-minded pursuit of this chimera has eroded civil liberties and human rights while shelving meaningful discussion of the root causes of terrorism: poverty, political exclusion and growing inequality. The world is a visibly more dangerous, less peaceful world as a result.

Muslim countries are boiling over with anger and resentment; fundamentalist, militant Islam is resurgent; and there are growing numbers of dead on all sides. A war without victory, with no end in sight. As the injustices in Iraq, Afghanistan, Pakistan, Chechnya and the West Bank simmer, hatred of the West grows, sympathy for jihad spreads and opposition to the West's globalization project strengthens.

Yet none of these recent maneuverings has altered the determination of critics to reshape globalization into a force for improving the lives of the majority of the world's people.

Across Latin America the electorate has embraced

democracy and said 'no' to a free trade model which has destroyed national economies, subverted local cultures and thrown millions into poverty and unemployment.

At the international level, despite rising tensions in the Middle East, there has been encouraging progress in building institutions which reinforce global citizenship and bolster international law – however imperfect. Among these achievements are the Kyoto Protocol on Climate Change, the UN Ban on Landmines, the International Tribunals on former Yugoslavia and Rwanda and the International Criminal Court.

Though the vocabulary is relatively new, the concept of globalization is as old as capitalism itself – a continuing saga of shifting markets and melding cultures. The world has been shrinking for centuries. Peppers, maize and potatoes, once found only in Latin America, are now common foods in India, Africa and Europe. Spices originally from Indonesia thrive in the Caribbean. The descendants of black Africans, first brought as slaves to work the land of the 'new world,' have become Americans, Jamaicans, Canadians, Brazilians and Guyanese.

But the 'old story' of globalization today has developed a new twist sparked by technological change. The micro-electronics revolution has irrevocably altered the essence of human communication. Digital technology has created a world of instant communications, creating what some have called the 'third wave' of economic growth.

The computer revolution that has boosted the new global economy has also been used in other, sometimes contradictory, ways. Images of conflict and violence can spread with lightening speed even as opponents of globalization use email and mobile phones to share information, strategize across international borders and organize demonstrations. The horrific torture of prisoners by US troops in Abu Ghraib prison; the stark videos of sobbing, frightened hostages in Iraq; the inflammatory Danish cartoons that sparked worldwide protests; the rise of the World Social Forum; the coordinated global demonstrations against the Iraq war; the proliferation of grassroots citizens' movements. All are in some way the fruits of globalization.

Just as technology can stoke the fires of dissent and amplify events which once might have remained unknown, so the speed of global travel has turned the whole world into ground zero for lethal, new diseases. The deadly SARS epidemic in 2003 reached 31 countries in less than a month. The World Health Organization predicts that the avian flu virus, once it crosses to humans, could kill up to seven million people worldwide. The globalization of trade and the industrialization of animal husbandry are intimately linked to the spread of these potential pandemics.

There is every reason to believe this global exchange of people, products, plants, animals, technologies and ideas will continue. The process of change is unstoppable. And despite the dangers it holds much promise, containing the seeds of a better future. If we jointly recognize the common thread of humanity that ties us together then how can globalization not be a positive force for change?

The Western tradition is steeped in optimism and the notion of progress. Growth is held up by some as the measure of human development and the vision of a globally unified market is the ultimate goal. The expansion of trade in goods and services between countries is said to be the key to a more equal, more peaceful, less parochial world. Eventually, so the argument goes, global integration and cross-cultural understanding will result in a borderless world where narrow political interests are put aside in a new pact of shared universal humanity.

This is a compelling vision. We live in a world of enormous wealth and great opportunity. There are now more people living longer, healthier, more productive lives than at any time in human history. And much of that is due to the extraordinary capacity of industrial capitalism to produce the goods.

But this success has been compromised by a corporate-led plan for economic integration which threatens cultural uniqueness, economic independence and political sovereignty. Instead of helping build a better world for all, the fundamentalist free-market model is eroding both democracy and equity. The social goals, the cohesive values that make us work as communities, are being ignored in the headlong rush to break down the barriers to global trade.

Gaps between rich and poor are widening, decision-making power is concentrated in fewer and fewer hands, local cultures are wiped out, biological diversity is destroyed, regional tensions are increasing and the environment is nearing the point of collapse. That is the sad reality of globalization, an opportunity for human progress whose great potential has been thwarted. Instead we have a global economic system which feeds on itself while marginalizing the fundamental human needs of people and communities.

This *No-Nonsense Guide* sketches the picture of that global economic system – its history, its structure, its failings – and the forces in whose interest it works. By understanding how we got here and what is at stake perhaps we can find a route out of our current impasse. The solutions are by no means definite. But there is a lively debate and change is in the wind. I hint at some of these ideas in the final chapter.

The hard facts are clear: unless we begin to alter the current global economic system, and soon, the tangible benefits of globalization will be swamped by a rising tide of inequality and injustice.

Wayne Ellwood
Toronto, March 2006

1 Globalization then and now

Globalization is a new word which describes an old process: the integration of the global economy that began in earnest with the launch of the European colonial era five centuries ago. But the process has accelerated over the past 30 years with the explosion of computer technology, the dismantling of barriers to the movement of goods and capital, and the expanding political and economic power of multinational corporations.

MORE THAN FIVE centuries ago, in a world without electricity, cell phones, refrigeration, DVDs, the internet, automobiles, airplanes or nuclear weapons, one man had a foolish dream. Or so it seemed at the time. Cristóbal Colón, an ambitious young Genoese sailor and adventurer, was obsessed with Asia – a region about which he knew nothing, apart from unsubstantiated rumors of its colossal wealth. Such was the strength of his obsession (some say his greed) that he was able to convince the King and Queen of Spain to finance a voyage into the unknown across a dark, seemingly limitless expanse of water then known as the Ocean Sea. His goal: to find the Grand Khan of China and the gold that was reportedly there in profusion.

Centuries later Colón would become familiar to millions of school children across the West as Christopher Columbus, the famous 'discoverer' of the Americas. In fact, the 'discovery' was more of an accident. The intrepid Columbus never did reach Asia, not even close. Instead, after five weeks at sea, he found himself sailing under a tropical sun into the turquoise waters of the Caribbean, making his landfall somewhere in the Bahamas, which he promptly named San Salvador (the Savior). The place clearly delighted Columbus' weary crew. They loaded up with fresh water and unusual foodstuffs. And they were befriended by the island's indigenous population, the Taino.

'They are the best people in the world and above all the gentlest,' Columbus wrote in his journal. 'They very willingly showed my people where the water was, and they themselves carried the full barrels to the boat, and took great delight in pleasing us. They became so much our friends that it was a marvel.'[1]

Twenty years and several voyages later, most of the Taino were dead and the other indigenous peoples of the Caribbean were either enslaved or under attack. Globalization, even then, had moved quickly from an innocent process of cross-cultural exchange to a nasty scramble for wealth and power. As local populations died off from European diseases or were literally worked to death by their captors, thousands of European colonizers followed. Their desperate quest was for gold and silver. But the conversion of heathen souls to the Christian faith gave an added fillip to their plunder. Eventually European settlers colonized most of the new lands to the north and south of the Caribbean.

Columbus' adventure in the Americas was notable for many things, not least his focus on extracting as much wealth as possible from the land and the people. But more importantly his voyages opened the door to 450 years of European colonialism. And it was this centuries-long imperial era that laid the groundwork for today's global economy.

Old globalization
Although globalization has become a commonplace term in recent years, many people would be hard-pressed to define what it actually means. The lens of history provides a useful beginning. Globalization is an age-old process and one firmly rooted in the experience of colonialism. One of Britain's most famous imperial spokesmen, Cecil Rhodes, put the case for

colonialism succinctly in the 1890s. 'We must find new lands,' he said, 'from which we can easily obtain raw materials and at the same time exploit the cheap slave labor that is available from the natives of the colonies. The colonies [will] also provide a dumping ground for the surplus goods produced in our factories.'[2]

During the colonial era European nations spread their rule across the globe. The British, French, Dutch, Spanish, Portuguese, Belgians, Germans, and later the Americans, took possession of most of what was later called the Third World. And of course they also expanded into Australia, New Zealand/Aotearoa and North America. In some places (the Americas, Australia, New Zealand and southern Africa) they did so with the intent of establishing new lands for European settlement. Elsewhere (Africa and Asia) their interest was more in the spirit of Rhodes' vision: markets and plunder. From 1600-1800 incalculable riches were siphoned out of Latin America to become the chief source of finance for Europe's industrial revolution.

Global trade expanded rapidly during the colonial period as European powers sucked in raw materials from their new dominions: furs, timber and fish from Canada; slaves and gold from Africa; sugar, rum and fruits from the Caribbean; coffee, sugar, meat, gold and silver from Latin America; opium, tea and spices from Asia. Ships crisscrossed the oceans. Heading towards the colonies their holds were filled with settlers and manufactured goods; returning home the stout galleons and streamlined clippers bulged with coffee, copra and cocoa. By the 1860s and the 1870s world trade was booming. It was a 'golden era' of international commerce – though the European powers pretty much stacked things in their favor. Wealth from their overseas colonies flooded into France, England, Holland and Spain but some of it also flowed back into the colonies as investment – into railways, roads,

Tyranny and poverty

Colonialism in the Americas separated Indians from their land, destroyed traditional economies and left native people among the poorest of the poor.

- The Spanish ran the Bolivian silver mines with a slave labor system known as the mita; nearly eight million Indians had died in the Potosí mines by 1650.
- Suicide and alcoholism are common responses to social dislocation. Suicide rates on Canadian Indian reserves are 10 to 20 times higher than the national average.
- In Guatemala life expectancy for non-natives is 61 years; for Indians it is 45. The infant mortality rate for Indian children is twice that of non-Indians (160 deaths per thousand versus 80). ■

Indian Population of the Americas: 1492 and 1992

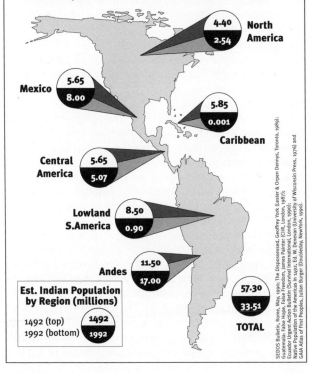

North America 4.40 / 2.54

Mexico 5.65 / 8.00

Caribbean 5.85 / 0.001

Central America 5.65 / 5.07

Lowland S.America 8.50 / 0.90

Andes 11.50 / 17.00

TOTAL 57.30 / 33.51

Est. Indian Population by Region (millions)

1492 (top)
1992 (bottom)

SEDOS Bulletin, Rome, May, 1990; The Dispossessed, Geoffrey York (Lester & Orpen Dennys, Toronto, 1989); Guatemala: False Hope, False Freedom, James Painter (CIIR, London, 1987); Ecuador Urgent Action Bulletin (Survival International, London, 1990); Native Population of the Americas in 1492, Ed. W. Denevan (University of Wisconsin Press, 1976) and GAIA Atlas of First Peoples, Julian Burger (Doubleday, NewYork, 1990).

ports, dams and cities. Such was the range of global commerce in the 19th century that capital transfers from North to South were actually greater at the end of the 1890s than at the end of the 1990s. By 1913 exports (one of the hallmarks of increasing economic integration) accounted for a larger share of global production than they did in 1999.

When people talk about globalization today they're still talking mostly about economics, about an expanding international trade in goods and services based on the concept of 'comparative advantage'. This theory was first developed in 1817 by the British economist David Ricardo in his *Principles of Political Economy and Taxation*. Ricardo wrote that nations should specialize in producing goods in which they have a natural advantage and thereby find their market niche. He believed this would benefit both buyer and seller but only if certain conditions were maintained, such as: 1) trade between partners must be balanced so that one country doesn't become indebted and dependent on another; and 2) investment capital must be anchored locally and not allowed to flow from a high-wage country to a low-wage country. Unfortunately, in today's high-tech world of instant communications neither of these key conditions exists. The result: Ricardo's vision of local self-reliance mixed with balanced exports and imports is nowhere to be seen. Instead, export-led trade dominates the global economic agenda. Increasingly, the only route to growth is based on expanding exports to the rest of the world.

The rationale is that all countries and all peoples eventually benefit from the results of increased trade. And world trade has zoomed ahead in the last decade. It grew at an average 6.6 per cent during the 1990s and is set to grow at around 6 per cent a year over the next 10 years. Global trade is actually growing faster than total world output which saw increases of 3.2 per cent during the 1990s and may reach 3 per cent annually over the next decade. This expansion of trade is expected to increase global income by up to $500 billion early in this new millennium. Unfortunately, most of this wealth will end up in the hands of the industrialized nations. They account for the lion's share of world trade and they mostly trade with each other. Indeed, the rich world accounts for almost two-thirds of global merchandise exports, a figure which has remained more or less steady since 1960. The share of Latin America, Central and Eastern Europe and Africa in total world exports was lower in 2002 than in 1960.[3]

Nonetheless, the world has changed in the last century in ways that have completely altered the character of the global economy and its impact on people and the natural world. Today's globalization is vastly different from both the colonial era and the immediate post-World War Two period. Even arch-capitalists like currency speculator George Soros have voiced doubts about the negative values that underlie the direction of the modern global economy.

'Insofar as there is a dominant belief in our society today,' he writes, 'it is a belief in the magic of the marketplace. The doctrine of laissez-faire capitalism holds that the common good is best served by the uninhibited pursuit of self-interest... Unsure of what they stand for, people increasingly rely on money as the criterion of value... The cult of success has replaced a belief in principles. Society has lost its anchor.'

Market magic

The 'magic of the marketplace' is not a new concept. It's been around in one form or another since the father of modern economics, Adam Smith, first published his pioneering work *The Wealth of Nations* in 1776. Coincidentally, the same year Britain's 13 restless American colonies declared independence from the mother land. But Smith's concept of the market was a far cry from the one championed by today's globalization boosters. Smith was adamant that markets worked most efficiently when there was equality between buyer and seller, and when neither was large enough to influence the market price. This, he said, would ensure that all parties received a fair return and that society as a whole would benefit through the best use of its natural and human resources. Smith also believed that capital was best invested locally so that owners could see what was happening with their investment and could have hands-on management of its use. Author and activist David Korten sums up Smith's thinking as follows:

'His vision of an efficient market was one composed of small owner-managed enterprises located in the communities where the owners resided. Such owners would share in the community's values and have a personal stake in its future. It is a market that has little in common with a globalized economy, dominated by

Driving growth

International trade is expanding faster than the world's economic output. This trade is seen as one of the main 'engines' of economic growth. ■

World Trade Organization www.wto.org

Growth in the volume of world merchandise trade and GDP, 1994-2004 (Annual percentage change)

massive corporations without local or national allegiance, managed by professionals who are removed from real owners by layers of investment institutions and holding companies.'[4]

As Korten hints, the world we live in today is vastly different from the one that Adam Smith inhabited. Take the communications technology revolution since 1980. In barely 25 years computers, fiber-optics, satellites and microprocessors have radically altered the production, sales and distribution of goods and services as well as patterns of global investment. Coupled with improvements in air freight and ocean transport, companies can now move their plants and factories to wherever costs are lowest. Being close to the target market is no longer crucial. Improved technology and relatively inexpensive oil (for the moment anyway) has led to a massive increase in goods being transported by air and sea. World air traffic cargo tripled from 1985 to 1997 and is predicted to triple again by 2015. The Council of the International Civil Aviation Organization (ICAO) notes that about 2 billion passengers and 44 million tons of freight were carried by the world's airlines in 2005, a 44 and 74 per cent increase respectively over 10 years. The global shipping business which now consumes more than 140 million tons of fuel oil a year is expected to increase by 85 per cent in the next decade. And costs are falling too. According to the Washington-based World Shipping Council in 2004, 7,241 individual vessels made more than 72,000 US port calls. In the last 15 years, rates on the three major US trade shipping routes have fallen by between 23 and 46 per cent. In 2000, American exporters spent about $3 billion less than they did in 1985 to ship their goods to market – extraordinary considering inflation rose 65 per cent in that same period.

It's estimated that ocean freight unit costs have fallen 70 per cent since the 1980s while air freight costs have fallen three to four per cent a year on average over the last two decades.

These cheap transport rates in reality are 'cheap' only in a purely financial sense. They reflect 'internal' costs – the costs of packaging, marketing, labor, debt and profit. But they don't reflect the 'external' impact on the environment of this massive use of irreplaceable fossil fuels. Moving more goods around the planet increases pollution, contributes to ground-level ozone (ie smog) and boosts greenhouse gas emissions, a major source of global warming and climate change. These environmental costs are basically ignored in the profit and loss equation of business. This is one of the main reasons environmentalists object to the globalization of trade. Companies make the profits but society has to foot the bill.

The other key factor which makes globalization today so different has to do with structural changes to the world economy since the early 1970s. It was then that the system of rules set up at the end of World War Two to manage global trade collapsed. The fixed currency-exchange regime agreed at Bretton Woods, New Hampshire, in 1944 gave the world 35 years of relatively steady economic growth.

Pinball capital

Short-term speculative capital whizzes around the world leaving ravaged economies and human devastation in its wake. East Asia (Indonesia, South Korea, Thailand, Malaysia, the Philippines) suffered a destructive net reversal of private capital flows from 1996 to 1997 of $12 billion.

Percentage change in GDP before and after the Asian financial crisis

	Thailand	Indonesia	Malaysia	S.Korea
Average 1980-90	7.6	6.1	5.2	9.4
Average 1990-96	8.3	7.7	8.7	7.3
Average 1997	-7	-16	-6	-6

Human Development Report 1999, UN Development Program / Oxford University Press; Financial Frenzy, Liberalization, Speculation and Regulation, War on Want, London 1999.

But around 1980 things began to change with the emergence of fundamentalist free-market governments in Britain and the US; and the later disintegration of the state-run command economy in the former Soviet Union. The formula for economic progress adopted by the administrations of Margaret Thatcher in the UK and Ronald Reagan in the US called for a drastic reduction in the regulatory role of the state. According to their intellectual influences, Austrian economist Friedrich Hayek and University of Chicago academic Milton Friedman, meddlesome big government was the problem. Instead, government was to take its direction from the market. Companies must be free to move their operations anywhere in the world to minimize costs and maximize returns to investors. Free trade, unfettered investment, deregulation, balanced budgets, low inflation and privatization of publicly-owned enterprises were trumpeted as the six-step plan to national prosperity.

The deregulation of world financial markets went hand-in-hand with an emphasis on free trade. Banks, insurance companies and investment dealers, whose operations had been mostly confined within national

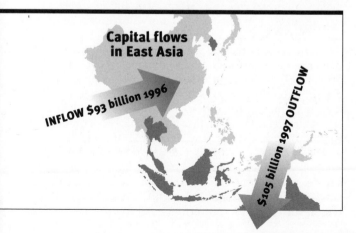

Capital flows in East Asia

INFLOW $93 billion 1996

$105 billion 1997 OUTFLOW

borders, were suddenly unleashed. Within a few years the big players from Europe, Japan and North America expanded into each other's markets as well as into the newly-opened and fragile financial services markets in the Global South. Aided by sophisticated computer systems (which made it easy to transfer huge amounts of money instantly) and governments desperate for investment, the big banks and investment houses were quick to invest surplus cash anywhere they could turn a profit. In this new relaxed atmosphere finance capital became a profoundly destabilizing influence on the global economy.

Instead of long-term investment in the production of real goods and services, speculators in the global casino make money from money – with little concern for the impact of their investments on local communities or national economies. Governments everywhere now fear the destabilizing impact of this 'hot money'. Recent United Nations (UN) studies show a direct correlation between the frequency of financial crises around the world and the huge increase in international capital flows during the 1990s.

The collapse of the East Asian currencies, which began in July 1997, was a catastrophic example of the damage caused by nervous short-term investors. Until then the 'Tiger Economies' of Thailand, Taiwan, Singapore, Malaysia and South Korea had been the success stories of globalization. Advocates of open markets pointed to these countries as proof that classic capitalism would bring wealth and prosperity to millions in the developing world – though they conveniently ignored the fact that in all these countries the State took a strong and active role in shaping the economy. According to dissident ex-World Bank Chief Economist, Joseph Stiglitz: 'The combination of high savings rates, government investment in education and state-directed industrial policy all served to make the region an economic powerhouse. Growth rates were

Third World

If there's a Third World, then there must be a First and Second World too. When the term was first coined in 1952 by the French demographer, Alfred Sauvy, there was a clear distinction, though the differences have become blurred over the past decade. Derived from the French phrase, *tiers monde*, the term was first used to suggest parallels between the *tiers monde* (the world of the poor countries) and the *tiers état* (the third estate or common people of the French revolutionary era). The First World was the North American/European 'Western bloc' while the Soviet-led 'Eastern bloc' was the Second World. These two groups had most of the economic and military power and faced off in a tense ideological confrontation commonly called the 'Cold War'. Third World countries in Africa, Latin America, Asia and the Pacific had just broken free of colonial rule and were attempting to make their own way rather than become entangled in the tug-of-war between East and West. Since the break-up of the Soviet Union in the early 1990s the term Third World has less meaning and its use is diminishing. Now many refer to the 'developing nations', the Majority World or just the South. ■

phenomenal for decades and the standard of living rose enormously for tens of millions of people.'[5]

Foreign investment was tightly controlled by national governments until the early 1990s, severely in South Korea and Taiwan, less so in Thailand and Malaysia. Then as a result of continued pressure from the International Monetary Fund (IMF) and others, the 'tigers' began to open up their capital accounts and private sector businesses began to borrow heavily.

Spectacular growth rates floated on a sea of foreign investment as offshore investors poured dollars into the region, eager to harvest double-digit returns. In 1996 capital was flowing into East Asia at almost $100 billion a year. But mostly the cash went into risky real estate ventures or onto the local stock market where it inflated share prices far beyond the value of their underlying assets.

In Thailand, where the Asian 'miracle' first began to sour, over-investment in real estate left the market glutted with $20 billion worth of new unsold properties. The house of cards collapsed when foreign investors began to realize that Thai financial institutions to which they had lent billions could not meet loan repayments. Spooked by the specter of falling profits and a stagnant real estate market, investors called in their loans and cashed in their investments – first slowly, then in a panic-stricken rush.

More than $105 billion left the entire region in the next 12 months, equivalent to 11 per cent of the domestic output of the most seriously affected countries – Indonesia, the Philippines, South Korea, Thailand and Malaysia.[6] Having abandoned any kind of capital controls, Asian governments were powerless to stop the massive hemorrhage of funds. Ironically, the IMF's 1997 *Annual Report*, written just before the crisis, had singled out Thailand's 'remarkable economic performance' and 'consistent record of sound macroeconomic policies'.

The IMF was to be proven wrong – disastrously so. Across the region economic output plummeted while unemployment soared, leaping by a factor of ten in Indonesia alone. The human costs of the East Asian economic crisis were immediate and devastating. As bankruptcies soared, firms shut their doors and millions of workers were laid off. More than 400 Malaysian companies declared bankruptcy between July 1997 and March 1998 while in Indonesia – the poorest country affected by the crisis – 20 per cent of the population, nearly 40 million people, were pushed into poverty. The impact of the economic slowdown had the devastating effect of reducing both family income and government expenditures on social and health services for years afterwards. In Thailand, more than 100,000 children were yanked from school when parents could no longer afford tuition fees. The crash also had a knock-on effect outside Asia. Shock-waves rippled through Latin America, nearly tipping Brazil into recession while the Russian economy suffered worse damage. Growth rates slipped into reverse and the Russian ruble became nearly worthless as a medium of international exchange.

The East Asian crisis was a serious blow to the 'promise' of globalization – and a stiff challenge to the orthodox economic prescriptions of the IMF. Across the region, the Fund was reviled as the source of economic disaster. The citizens of East Asia saw their interests ignored in favor of Western banks and investors. In the end, writes Stiglitz: 'It was the IMF policies which undermined the market as well as the long-run stability of the economy and society.' It was the first time that the 'global managers' and finance kingpins showed that the system wasn't all it was made out to be. The world economy was more fragile, and thus more explosive, than anybody had imagined. As the region slowly recovered, citizens around the world began to scratch their heads and wonder about the pros and cons of globalization, especially the wisdom of unregulated investment. The mass public protests against the WTO, the IMF/World Bank and the G8 were still to come – in Seattle, Prague, Genoa, Quebec City, Doha and elsewhere. But the East Asian crisis planted real seeds of doubt about the merits of corporate globalization.

1 *The Conquest of Paradise: Christopher Columbus and the Columban Legacy,* Kirkpatrick Sale (Knopf, New York 1990). **2** *The Ecologist,* Vol 29, No 3, May/June 1999. **3** *Development and Globalization: Facts and Figures 2004,* UNCTAD. **4** *When Corporations Rule the World,* David Korten (Kumarian/Berrett-Koehler, West Hartford/San Francisco, 1995). **5** *Globalization and its Discontents,* Joseph Stiglitz (WW Norton, New York/London, 2003). **6** *Human Development Report 1999* (United Nations Development Program, New York/Oxford, 1999).

2 The Bretton Woods Trio

The Great Depression of the 1930s leads to the birth of Keynesianism and the interventionist state. As World War Two ends, the victors put together a new set of rules for the global economy. This postwar financial architecture includes the World Bank, the International Monetary Fund (IMF) and the General Agreement on Tariffs and Trade (GATT). But as Third World nations emerge from centuries of colonialism these institutions are seen increasingly as pillars of the status quo.

AS WORLD WAR TWO was drawing to a close, the world's leading politicians and government officials, mostly from the victorious 'Allied' nations (mainly Britain, the United States, the Soviet Union, Canada, France, Australia and New Zealand) began to think about the need to establish a system of rules to run the postwar global economy.

Before the widespread outbreak of the war in 1939 trading nations everywhere had been racked by a crippling economic depression. When the US stock market crashed in October 1929 the shockwaves were felt around the world. Nations turned inward in an attempt to pull themselves out of a steep economic skid. But without a system of global rules there was no coherence or larger logic to the 'beggar-thy-neighbor' polices adopted worldwide. High tariff barriers were thrown up between countries with the result that world trade nose-dived, economic growth spluttered and mass unemployment and poverty followed. From 1929 to 1932 global trade fell by an astounding 62 per cent while global industrial production slumped by 36 per cent. As a result the 1930s became a decade of radical politics and rancorous social ferment in the West as criticism of laissez-faire capitalism and an unchecked market economy grew.

Scholars like Hungarian exile Karl Polanyi helped reinforce a growing suspicion of a market-based economic model which put money and investors at the center of its concerns rather than social values and human well-being. 'To allow the market mechanism to be the sole director of the fate of human beings and their natural environment... would result in the demolition of society,' Polanyi wrote in his masterwork, *The Great Transformation.*

Polanyi was not alone in his distrust of the market economy. Other thinkers like the influential British economist John Maynard Keynes were also grappling with a way of controlling global markets, making them work for people and not the other way around. Keynes both admired and feared the power of the market system. With the example of the Great Depression of the 1930s fresh in his mind he predicted that, without firm boundaries and controls, capitalism would be immobilized by its own greed, and would eventually self-destruct. As it happened only World War Two turned things around. The War set the factories and farms humming again as millions of troops were deployed by all sides in the conflict. Armaments manufacturers, aircraft factories and other military suppliers ran 24-hour shifts, primed by government spending. Then, as the War wound down, government policy makers began to think about how to ensure a smooth transformation to a peacetime economy.

It was Keynes' radical notion of an 'interventionist' state to which governments turned in an effort to set their economies back on a steady keel. Until the worldwide slump of the 1930s the accepted economic wisdom had been that a degree of unemployment was a 'normal condition' of the free market. The economy might go up and down according to the business cycle but in the long run growth (and increased global trade) would create new jobs and sop up the unemployed.

Keynes was skeptical of this *laissez-faire* orthodoxy, suggesting that the economy was a human-made artifact and that people acting together through their government could have some control over its direction. Why not act now, he suggested, since 'in the long run we're all dead.' His approach offered a way out for governments who found themselves helplessly mired in economic stagnation.

In *The General Theory of Employment, Interest and Money* published in 1936, Keynes argued that the free market, left on its own, actually creates unemployment. Profitability, he said, depends on suppressing wages and cutting costs by replacing labor with technology. In other words, profits and a certain amount of unemployment go hand-in-hand – so far so good, at least for those making the profits. But Keynes went on to show that lowering wages and laying off workers would inevitably result in fewer people who could afford to buy the goods that factories were producing. As demand fell, so would sales; factory owners would be forced to lay off even more workers. This, reasoned Keynes, was the start of a downward spiral with terrible human consequences.

To 'prime the economic pump' Keynes suggested governments intervene actively in the economy. He reasoned that business owners and rich investors are unlikely to open their wallets if the prospects for growth look dim. When the economy is in a tailspin then it is up to government to step in – by spending on public goods (education, health care, job training) and on 'infrastructure' (roads, dams, trams and railways). And by giving direct financial support to the unemployed.

Even if governments had to go into debt to kick-start growth Keynes advised politicians not to worry. The price was worth it. By directly stimulating the economy, government could rekindle demand and help reverse the downward spiral. Soon companies would begin to invest again to increase production to meet the growing demand. This would mean hiring more workers who would soon have more money in their pockets. As jobs increased so would taxes. Eventually, the government would be able to pay back its debt from increased tax revenues raised from a now healthy, growing economy.

Desperate Western governments were quick to adopt the 'Keynesian' solution to economic stagnation. In the US the 'New Deal' policies of the Roosevelt administration were directly influenced by Keynes. The American Employment Act of 1946 accepted the federal government's responsibility 'to promote maximum employment, production and purchasing power'. The British Government, too, in 1944 accepted as one of its primary aims 'the maintenance of a high and stable level of employment after the war.'

Other countries like Canada, Australia and Sweden quickly followed. Keynes' influence spread and people began to believe that economics was finally a manageable science in the service of human progress.

'We are witnessing a development under which the economic system ceases to lay down the law to society and the primacy of society over that system is secured.' Thus wrote Polanyi in a moment of supreme optimism just before the end of the war.

Bretton Woods
It was this confidence that delegates from 44 nations brought to the postcard-pretty New England resort village of Bretton Woods in July 1944. The aim of the UN Monetary and Financial Conference was to erect a new framework for the postwar global economy – a stable, cooperative international monetary system which would promote national sovereignty and prevent future financial crises. The purpose was not to bury capitalism but to save it. The main proposal was for a system of fixed exchange rates. In the light of the

Depression of the previous decade floating rates were now seen as inherently unstable and destructive of national development plans.

Keynes' influence at Bretton Woods was huge. But despite his lobbying and cajoling he did not win the day on every issue. The US opposed his 'soft' approach and in the end the enormous military and economic clout of the Americans proved impossible to overcome.

The Conference rejected his proposals to establish a world 'reserve currency' administered by a global central bank. Keynes believed this would have created a more stable and fairer world economy by automatically recycling trade surpluses to finance trade deficits. Both deficit and surplus nations would take responsibility for trade imbalances. However his solution did not fit the interests of the US, eager to take on the role of the world's economic powerhouse. Instead the Conference opted for a system based on the free movement of goods with the US dollar as the international currency. The dollar was linked to gold and the price of gold was fixed at $35 an ounce (28g). In effect the US dollar became 'as-good-as-gold' and in this one act became the dominant currency of international exchange.

Three governing institutions emerged from the gathering to oversee and coordinate the global economy. These were not neutral economic mechanisms: they contained a powerful bias in favor of global competition and corporate enterprise. And each had a distinct role to play.

1 The International Monetary Fund (IMF)
The IMF was born with a mission: to create economic stability for a world which had just been through the trauma of depression and the devastation of war. As originally conceived it was supposed to 'facilitate the expansion and balanced growth of international trade'

and 'to contribute to the promotion and maintenance of high levels of employment and real income'.

A major part of its job was to oversee a system of 'fixed' exchange rates. The aim was to stop countries from devaluing their national currencies to get a competitive edge over their neighbors – a defining feature of the economic chaos of the 1930s.

The Fund was also to promote currency 'convertibility' to encourage world trade – to make it easier to exchange one currency for another when trading across national borders.

And finally the new agency was to act as a 'lender-of-last-resort' supplying emergency loans to countries which ran into short-term cash flow problems. Keynes' idea was to set up an International Clearing Union which would automatically provide unconditional loans to countries experiencing balance-of-payments problems. These loans would be issued 'no strings attached' with the purpose of supporting domestic demand and maintaining employment. Otherwise countries feeling the pinch would be forced to balance their deficit by cutting off imports and lowering domestic demand and wages in favor of exports.

Keynes argued that international trade was a two-way street and that the 'winners' (those countries in surplus) were as obligated as the 'losers' (those countries in deficit) to bring the system back to balance. Keynes suggested that pressure be brought to bear on surplus nations so they would be forced to increase their imports and recycle the surplus to deficit nations.

But Keynes' view did not prevail. Instead a proposal put forward by US Treasury Secretary Harry Dexter White became the basis for the IMF. The International Clearing Union idea disappeared. IMF members would not automatically receive loans when they tumbled into deficit. Instead members would have access to limited loan amounts which were to be determined by a complex quota system. Voting power within the IMF would be based on the level of financial contributions – one dollar, one vote – which meant that rich countries would call the shots.

When a country joins the IMF it is assigned a quota which is calculated in Special Drawing Rights (SDRs), the Fund's own unit of account. Quotas are assigned according to a country's relative position in the world economy which means that the most powerful economies have the most influence and clout. The US for example has the largest SDR quota at about 27 billion. The size of a member's quota determines a lot, including how many votes it has in IMF deliberations and how much foreign exchange it has access to if it runs into choppy financial waters.

Nonetheless, the IMF was founded on the belief that collective action was necessary to stabilize the global economy just as nations needed to unite together at the UN to stabilize the global political system.

The final decision was that balance-of-payments loans are contracted at less than the prevailing interest rate and members are supposed to use and repay them within five years. The issue of whether the IMF could attach conditions to these loans was unclear in the original Bretton Woods agreement. But Harry Dexter White was very clear six months later when he wrote in the journal *Foreign Affairs* that the Fund would not simply dole out money to debtor countries. The IMF would force countries to take measures which under the old gold standard (see p 36) would have happened automatically.

The delegates at the Bretton Woods Conference supported a gradual reduction of trade barriers and tariffs. But they were less enthusiastic about allowing the free movement of capital internationally.

Keynes, Britain's delegate to the meeting, advocated a balanced world trade system with strict controls on the movement of capital across borders. He held that the free movement of all goods and capital, advocated most powerfully by the US delegation, would inevitably lead to inequalities and instabilities.

2 The World Bank (International Bank for Reconstruction and Development)

One of the other key goals of the Bretton Woods Conference was to find a way to rebuild the economies of those nations that had been devastated by World War Two. The International Bank for Reconstruction and Development (IBRD) was created to spearhead this effort. The Bank is funded by dues from its members and by money borrowed on international capital markets. It makes loans to members below rates available at commercial banks. Its initial mandate was to provide loans for 'infrastructure' which included things like power plants, dams, roads, airports, ports, agricultural development and education systems. The Bank poured money into reconstruction in Europe after World War Two. But it was not enough to satisfy the United States whose booming industries were in need of viable markets. In response the US set up its own Marshall Plan, named after then US Secretary of State, George Marshall. From April 1948 to December 1951 the US provided $12.5 billion to 16 European nations, largely in the form of grants rather than loans.

As Europe gradually recovered, the IBRD turned from 'reconstruction' to 'development' in the newly-independent countries of the Third World where it became widely known as the World Bank. As Southern countries sought to enter the industrial age the Bank became a major player throughout the region. According to the 'stages of growth' economic theory popular at the time, developing nations could achieve economic 'take-off' only from a strong infrastructure 'runway'. It was part of the Bank's self-defined role to build this 'infrastructural capacity' and this it did enthusiastically by funding dams, hydroelectric projects and highway systems throughout Latin America, Asia and Africa.

But despite the Bank's low lending rates it was clear early on that the very poorest countries would have difficulty meeting loan repayments. So in the late 1950s the Bank was pressured into setting up the International Development Association (IDA). This wing of the Bank was to provide 'soft loans' with very low interest or none at all – and so head off attempts by the emerging Third World countries to set up an independent aid agency, under UN auspices, separate from the Bretton Woods institutions. The Bank also established two other departments: the International Finance Corporation, which supports private-sector investment in Bank-approved projects, and the Multilateral Insurance Guarantee Agency, which provides risk insurance to foreign corporations and individuals who decide to invest in one of the Bank's member countries.

3 General Agreement on Tariffs and Trade (GATT)/ World Trade Organization (WTO)

Although the Bretton Woods agreement called for an International Trade Organization there was no consensus. The Americans balked at the idea that trade should be linked to employment policy or that Third World producers should get a fairer price for their commodity exports. So the GATT emerged in 1947 to set rules on global trade in industrial goods only. Its aim was to reduce national trade barriers and to stop the competitive, beggar-thy-neighbor trade policies that had so hobbled the global economy prior to World War Two. After seven rounds of tariff negotiations over the next 40 years GATT members reduced tariffs from 40-50 per cent to 4-5 per cent.

The final 'Uruguay Round' began in 1986. In March 1994, following its completion, politicians and bureaucrats met in Marrakech, Morocco, to approve a new World Trade Organization to replace the more loosely-structured GATT. The WTO, unlike the GATT, has the official status of an international organization rather than a treaty. Unlike the Bank and the Fund it does not set the rules. Instead it provides a forum for negotiations and then ensures that agreements are followed. By December 2005 it had 149 member states and 32 'observers'.

The WTO vastly expands GATT's mandate. The text of the WTO agreement had 26,000 pages: a hint of both its prolixity and its complexity. It includes the GATT agreements which mostly focus on trade in goods. But it also folds in the new General Agreement on Trade in Services (GATS) which potentially reduces barriers to investment in more than 160 areas – including basic needs like water, health care and education as well as telecommunications, banking and investment, transport and the environment. GATS is not a treaty. It's more like a framework agreement where negotiations can continue indefinitely. For large global corporations it's a potential goldmine of new

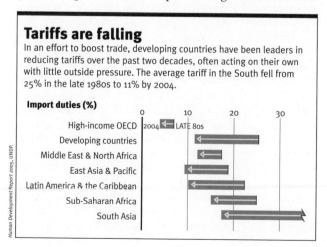

Tariffs are falling
In an effort to boost trade, developing countries have been leaders in reducing tariffs over the past two decades, often acting on their own with little outside pressure. The average tariff in the South fell from 25% in the late 1980s to 11% by 2004.

Import duties (%)

	0	10	20	30
High-income OECD	2004 ← LATE 80s			
Developing countries				
Middle East & North Africa				
East Asia & Pacific				
Latin America & the Caribbean				
Sub-Saharan Africa				
South Asia				

Human Development Report 2005, UNDP.

business opportunities.

From the outset GATT was seen as a 'rich man's club' dominated by Western industrial nations slow to concede their position of power. The WTO continues this tradition of rich world domination. Rubens Ricupero, former Secretary-General of the UN Conference on Trade and Development (UNCTAD) is frank in his assessment of the multilateral trading system. It is a matter of 'concrete evidence', he said at the September 1999 G77 (developing countries 'Group of 77') Ministerial Meeting in Morocco, that global trade rules are 'highly imbalanced and biased against developing countries'. Why is it, asks Ricupero, that developed countries have been given decades to 'adjust' their economies to imports of agricultural products and textiles from the Third World when poor countries are pressured to open

The gold standard

Until the Great Depression of the 1930s gold was the one precious metal that most large trading countries in the world recognized and accepted as a universal medium of exchange. The shift to gold began when international trade exploded after the industrial revolution. Britain was the first to adopt the gold standard in 1816; the US made the change in 1873 and by 1900 most of the world had joined them.

Most national currencies were redeemable in gold. Paper bank notes often contained the phrase 'the bank promises to pay the bearer on demand' the equivalent in gold. That implied you could go into a bank and demand the equivalent in gold if the mood moved you.

What that meant was that all nations set the value of their national currency in terms of ounces of gold (1 ounce = 28g). It was a convenient way of settling national trading accounts. And the fixed gold standard was supposed to both stabilize foreign exchange rates and domestic economies. A country's wealth could be measured by the amount of gold it had stored in its vaults; certainly an unfair advantage for those countries lucky enough to be sitting on vast natural deposits of gold.

With gold as a fixed standard the fluctuations of international trade were relatively simple to track. If a country's imports exceeded its exports then gold had to be shipped to those countries who were owed in order to balance the books. The decline in the amount of gold would then force a government their borders immediately to Western banks and telecommunication companies? As a case in point he mentions the multifiber arrangement (MFA) on textiles under which industrial countries were allowed to impose quotas restricting clothing and textile imports from developing nations. The MFA developed from a waiver which the US demanded on behalf of its domestic cotton industry in the late 1950s. By the time the MFA was finally phased out in January 2005 it had lasted nearly 50 years, a long time for a 'temporary' concession which was to allow US producers to adjust to cheap textile imports from abroad.[1]

In contrast, according to the UN Development Program (UNDP), developing countries have been much more willing to abandon import substitution policies and reduce trade barriers. The average tariff in developing countries fell from 25 per cent in the

---

to reduce the amount of cash in circulation. Because money was redeemable for gold both governments and banks would want to make sure they could cover themselves if necessary. Less money in circulation would tend to lower prices, dampening economic activity at home and decreasing imports. Gold flowing to countries on the receiving end would have the opposite effect. Governments would release more cash into the economy to cover the increase of gold in their vaults and prices would tend to increase.

With the Depression of the 1930s one country after another abandoned the gold standard in an attempt to 'devalue' their currencies to gain a 'competitive advantage' over their trading partners (ie to make their exports cheaper). There was an attempt to modify the gold link after World War Two when the US set the value of the dollar at $1/35$ of an ounce (0.9g) of gold but holders of cash were no longer able to demand gold in exchange and the circulation of gold coins was prohibited. Then in 1973 US President Richard Nixon suspended the exchange of American gold for foreign-held dollars at fixed rates. At that point gold became just another commodity, its price determined by the law of supply and demand. Many countries (as well as the International Monetary Fund) continue to hold vast gold reserves and quantities are occasionally sold on the open market – though sellers are careful not to flood the market and depress the international price too much. ■

late 1980s to 11 per cent by the end of 2004. India, for example, reduced its tariffs from an average of 82 per cent in 1990 to 30 per cent by the end of 2004. Brazil chopped average tariffs from 25 per cent to 12 per cent over the same period and China lowered them from 43 per cent in 1993 to 18 per cent four years later.

Notes UNDP: 'The world's highest trade barriers are erected against some of its poorest countries. On average trade barriers faced by developing countries exporting to rich countries are three to four times higher than those faced by rich countries when they trade with each other.'[2]

The WTO pursues its free trade agenda with the single-minded concentration of the true believer. Nonetheless there is a growing unease about the organization's globalizing agenda. Critics are especially wary of the Dispute Resolution Body (DRB) which gives the WTO the legal tools to approve tough trade sanctions by one member against another, especially on nations that might disagree with the organization's interpretation of global trade rules. Any member country, acting on behalf of a business with an axe to grind, can challenge the laws and regulations of another country on the grounds that they violate WTO rules.

Previously, if GATT wanted to discipline one of its members for not playing according to the rules every member had to agree. The WTO has considerably more power. The DRB appoints a panel of 'experts' who hear the case behind closed doors. If the panel decides on sanctions the only way to escape them is if they're opposed by every WTO member – a virtual impossibility. In effect the WTO regime is one of trade *über alles*. Environmental laws, labor standards, human rights legislation, public health policies, cultural protection, food self-reliance or any other policies held to be in the 'national interest' can be attacked as unfair 'impediments' to free trade.

Already there have been cases where the WTO has effectively struck down national legislation in its pursuit of a 'level playing field'. The 1999 WTO decision against the European Union (EU) over the importing of bananas is a case in point. The WTO's 'most favored nation' clause demands that similar products from different member countries be treated equally. Under the terms of the Lomé Convention (agreement) the EU had promised to give preference to bananas from former European colonies in Africa, the Caribbean and the Pacific. In general these banana growers tend to be small farmers who are less dependent on pesticide-intensive plantation methods than the giant US companies like Dole and Chiquita. Bananas account for about 60 per cent of export earnings in the Caribbean.

European view

The Europeans stressed their right to determine a sovereign foreign policy in relation to former colonies while the US argued that EU tariffs prohibited American banana companies in Latin America from reaching lucrative markets in Europe. The WTO decided on behalf of the US, ruling that the European preference was unfair. Meanwhile, small island nations in the Caribbean, so dependent on income from the banana trade, are worried the decision will wipe out their major export market in Britain and destroy their industry. They'll soon find out. Quotas on the import of 'third country' (ie Latin American) bananas into the EU were finally eliminated in January 2006.

All nations have the right to use the DRB to pursue their own economic self-interest. But the fact is that the world's major trading nations are also its most powerful economic actors. So the tendency is for the strong to use the new rules to dominate weaker countries. The 'national treatment clause' basically says that a country may not discriminate against products of foreign origin on any grounds whatsoever. And in so doing it removes the power of governments to develop economic policy which serves the moral, ethical or economic interests of their citizenry. WTO rules prohibit members from barring products if they disagree with the 'Processes and Methods of Production'. For example, if goods are produced by children in sweatshop conditions, well that's not really an issue. The same is true if a foreign factory fouls the air, if poverty wages are paid to the workers, or if the goods themselves are poisonous and dangerous.

According to WTO rules any country that refuses to import a product on the grounds that it may harm public health or damage the environment has to prove the case 'scientifically'. So Canada, the world's biggest asbestos producer, petitioned the WTO's dispute panel and won – forcing the EU to lift its ban on the import of the known carcinogen. And when the EU refused imports of hormone-fed beef from North America, the US took the case to the WTO arguing that there was no threat to human health from cows fed hormones. The EU ban on hormone-fed beef applied to their own farmers as well as foreign producers but that made little difference. The WTO panel decided in favor of the US, effectively ruling that Europeans had no right to pass laws that supported their opposition to hormones. The EU was ordered to compensate producers in the US and Canada for every year of lost export earnings. And in retaliation the WTO allowed the US to impose $116 million worth of sanctions on a range of European imports – including Dijon mustard, pork, truffles and Roquefort cheese.

Meanwhile, in 2001 the giant US-based shipping company, United Parcel Service (UPS), lodged a complaint with the North American Free Trade Agreement (NAFTA), which runs a dispute resolution body similar to the WTO, threatening Canada's government-run postal service. UPS charged that

Ottawa is unfairly subsidizing Canada Post and therefore poaching potential customers. In response the Council of Canadians and the Canadian Union of Postal Workers (CUPW) asked Ontario's Superior Court of Justice to rule that NAFTA's investment rules are unconstitutional.

According to Council Chair Maude Barlow, 'UPS claims that simply by having a public postal system, Canada is allowing unfair competition. By this logic, every public service from health care to education could face similar lawsuits. We don't intend to let foreign corporations destroy our public services.'

Meanwhile, in February 2006 the WTO ruled in favor of Canada, the US and Argentina in a dispute with the EU over genetically engineered crops. The WTO said that the EU discriminated against biotech seeds without adequate scientific evidence. US agribusiness says the ban costs American firms $300 million a year in sales to the EU. Critics, however, called the WTO decision a 'direct attack on democracy' – EU governments voted in 2005 to reaffirm their ban on GM seeds.[3]

And so it goes in the topsy-turvy world of economic globalization. Those institutions which first emerged from the Bretton Woods negotiations half a century ago have become more important players with each passing decade. It is their vision and their agenda which continue to shape the direction of the global economy. Together, they are fostering a model of liberalized trade and investment which is heartily endorsed by the world's biggest banks and corporations. A deregulated, privatized, corporate-led free market is the answer to humanity's problems, they tell us. The proof, though, is not so easily found.

1 'WTO must correct imbalances against South', Martin Khor, Third World Network Features, October 1999. **2** *Human Development Report 2005*, UNDP, New York, 2005. **3** 'Biotech industry gets boost', *Toronto Star*, 8 February 2006, p E3.

3 Debt and structural adjustment

Developing countries fight for a New International Economic Order, including fairer terms of trade, and push their case through UN agencies like UNCTAD and producer cartels like OPEC. Petrodollars flood Northern financial centers and President Nixon floats the dollar, sabotaging the Bretton Woods fixed exchange-rate system. When Third World debt expands the IMF and World Bank step in to bail out debt-strapped nations. In return they must adopt 'structural adjustment' policies which favor cheap exports and spread poverty throughout the South.

THE GLOBAL ECONOMY has changed dramatically since 1980. So it's hard to believe that it was only a decade or so before that the newly emerging colonies of Africa and Asia were joining with the nominally independent nations of Latin America to push for a 'new international economic order' (NIEO). Throughout the 1960s and early 1970s an insistent demand for radical change burst forth from the two-thirds of the world's people who lived outside the privileged circle of North America and Western Europe. There was a strong movement to shake off the legacy of colonialism and to fight for a new global system based on economic justice between nations. Some Third World states began to explore ways of increasing their bargaining power with the industrialized countries in Europe and North America by taking advantage of their control over key resources. The Organization of Petroleum Exporting Countries (OPEC) was formed in the early 1970s, hoping to control the supply of petroleum and ratchet up the price of oil, thereby increasing their share of global wealth and bringing prosperity to their populations. OPEC's success led to heady talk of 'producer cartels' to raise the price of other exports like sugar, coffee, cocoa, tin and rubber so that poor countries dependent on one or two primary commodities could gain more income and control over their own development. There was also strong vocal opposition to the growing power of Western-based corporations that were seen to be remaking the world in their own interests, trampling on the rights of weaker nations. When poor countries tried to increase the price of their primary exports they often found themselves confronting the near-monopoly control by big corporations of processing, distribution and marketing.

In the wake of OPEC, the NIEO was strongly endorsed at the Summit of Non-Aligned Nations in Algiers in September 1973. Then in April 1974 the Sixth Special Session of the UN adopted the *Declaration and Program of Action of the New International Economic Order*. The following December the General Assembly approved the *Charter of Economic Rights and Duties of States*.

Key NIEO demands included:

- 'Indexing' developing country export prices to tie them to the rising prices of manufactured exports from the developed nations.
- Hiking official development assistance to 0.7 per cent of GNP of the developed countries (a target which has still not been met today).
- Lowering tariffs on manufactured exports from the developing countries.
- Transferring technology to developing countries and separating the process from direct capital investment.

Meanwhile, the *Charter of Economic Rights and Duties of States* endorsed:

- The sovereignty of each country over its natural resources and economic activities, including the right to nationalize foreign property.
- The right of countries dependent on a small range of primary exports to form producer cartels.

- The declaration of principles for an NIEO was the culmination of a new 'solidarity of the oppressed' which had spread throughout the developing nations. Galvanized by centuries-old colonial injustices and sparked by the radical ideas of Franz Fanon in Algeria, Kwame Nkrumah in Ghana, Mahatma Gandhi in India, Sukarno in Indonesia, Julius Nyerere in Tanzania and Fidel Castro in Cuba, these 'Third World' nations set out to collectively challenge the entrenched power of the United States and Western Europe. The NIEO was not a grassroots movement. It was a collection of progressive intellectuals and politicians who believed correctly that, left on their own, free markets would never reduce global inequalities. Instead these leaders argued for improved 'terms of trade' and a more just international economic system. When bargaining failed, producer countries began to form trade alliances based on specific commodities.

Third World nations came together in political organizations like the Non-Aligned Movement which was initially an attempt to break out of the polarized East/West power struggle between the West and the Soviet Bloc. In the UN, developing countries formed the 'Group of 77' which was instrumental in creating the UN Conference on Trade and Development (UNCTAD). Within UNCTAD poor countries pushed for fairer 'terms of trade'. Many newly-independent countries of the South still relied heavily on the export of raw materials in the 1950s and 1960s. But there was a faltering effort and a stronger belief in the need to build local industrial capacities and to support the push for a 'new international economic order'. Why was it, they asked, that the price of everything they imported from the West, whether it was manufactured goods, spare parts or foodstuffs, seemed to creep ever upwards while the prices they received for their agricultural exports and raw materials remained the same – or even decreased? This patent injustice was one of the main concerns of the NIEO and the focus of its commodity program.

The idea was to intervene in the market, both to regulate supplies and steady prices to the benefit of producers and consumers. The ten core commodities were to be cocoa, coffee, tea, sugar, jute, cotton, rubber hard fibers, copper and tin. This new commodity system was to be based on 'international buffer stocks' with a 'common fund' to purchase these stocks, as well as new multilateral trade commitments and improved 'compensatory financing' to stabilize export earnings. Unfortunately, the NIEO was never really given much of a chance by Western nations who saw it as an erosion of their market advantage; while Third World nations were split by divergent interests and their lack of political power.

Transparent injustice

The transparent injustice of this enraged and frustrated leaders like Tanzania's Nyerere who referred to declining terms of trade as constantly 'riding the downward escalator'. Between 1980 and 1991 alone non-oil-exporting developing countries lost nearly $290 billion due to decreasing prices for their primary commodity exports. In response to this economic discrimination Third World nations also began agitating for an increase in 'untied' aid from the West; for more liberal terms on development loans; and for a quicker transfer of new manufacturing technologies from North to South.

In addition, most developing countries favored an active government role in running the national economy. They quite rightly feared that in a world of vast economic inequality they could easily be crushed between self-interested Western governments and their muscular business partners. That was the chief reason that many Third World nations began to take tentative steps to regulate foreign investment and to maintain at least minimal trade restrictions.

Debt and structural adjustment

This process began earlier in Latin America where nations began to encourage 'import substitution' in the 1950s as a way of boosting local manufacturing, employment and income. Countries like Brazil and Argentina used a mix of taxation policy, tariffs and financial incentives to attract both foreign and domestic investment. American and European auto companies set up factories to take advantage of import barriers. The development goal was to stimulate industrialization in order to produce goods locally and to boost export earnings. This had the added benefit of reducing imports, which both cut the need for scarce foreign exchange and kept domestic capital circulating inside the country. Unfortunately, the era of import substitution was short. Latin American nations were soon bullied into dismantling import barriers – foreign-made goods, mostly American, soon flooded in again so by the late 1980s there were few local producers of cars, TVs, fridges or other major household goods. Still, this was a brief but important step in trying to shift the balance of global power to poor countries.

The petrodollar boom

Even before the clamor for a new world economic order, momentous changes were beginning to unfold that would dramatically alter the fate of poor nations for decades to come. By the late 1960s the Bretton Woods dream of a stable monetary system of fixed exchange rates with the dollar as the only international currency was collapsing under the strain of American trade and budgetary deficits.

As the US war in Vietnam escalated, the Federal Reserve in Washington pumped out millions of dollars to finance the conflict. The US economy was firing on all cylinders and beginning to dangerously overheat. Inflation edged upwards while foreign debt ballooned to pay for the war.

World Bank President Robert McNamara also leapt

into the fray and contracted huge loans to the South during the 1970s – both for 'development' (essentially defined as basic infrastructure to bring 'backward' economies into the market system) and to act as a bulwark against a perceived worldwide communist threat. The Bank's stake in the South increased five-fold over the decade.

At the same time a guarded optimism took hold in the developing countries, fueled by moderately-high growth rates and a short-term boom in the price of primary commodities, particularly oil. The Organization of Petroleum Exporting Countries (OPEC) was the first, and ultimately the most successful, Third World 'producer union'. By standing together and controlling the supply of oil they were able to increase the price of petroleum three-fold to over $30 a barrel. The result was windfall surpluses for OPEC members – $310 billion for the period 1972-1977 alone. This 'oil shock' rippled through the global economy, triggering double-digit inflation and a massive currency 'recycling' problem.

What were OPEC nations to do with this vast new wealth of 'petrodollars'? Some of it they would spend on glittering new airports, power stations and other showcase mega-projects. But much of it eventually wound up as investment in Northern financial centers or deposited in Northern commercial banks. This was the birth of the 'eurocurrency' market – a huge pool of cash held outside the borders of the countries that originally issued the currency. The US dollar was the main 'eurocurrency' but there were also francs, guilders, marks and pounds.

Western banks, flush with this new OPEC money, began to search for borrowers. They didn't have long to look. Soon millions in loans were contracted to non-oil-producing Third World governments desperate to pay escalating fuel bills and to fund ambitious development goals. At the same time the massive increase in oil prices helped inflation soar around the world. Prices skyrocketed while growth slowed to a crawl and a new word was added to the lexicon of economists: 'stagflation'. In the midst of this economic chaos US President Richard Nixon moved unilaterally to de-link the dollar from gold. As a result the world moved to a system of floating exchange rates. Nixon also devalued the greenback (US dollar) against other major world currencies and jacked up interest rates to attract investment; both moves had an enormous impact on the global economy.

By slashing the value of the dollar Washington effectively reduced the huge debt it owed to the rest of the world. The US had been running a massive deficit to pay the costs of the war in Vietnam. As interest rates shot up, those countries reeling under OPEC oil-price hikes had the cost of their eurodollar loans (most of which were denominated in US dollars) double and even triple, almost overnight. The debt of the non-oil producing Third World increased five-fold between 1973 and 1982, reaching a staggering $612 billion. The banks were desperate to lend to meet their interest obligations on deposits, so easy terms were the order of the day. Dictators who could exact payments from their cowering populations with relative ease must have seemed like a good bet for lenders looking for a secure return.

Sometimes the petrodollar loan money was squandered on grandiose and ill-considered projects. Sometimes it was simply filched – siphoned off by Third World élites into personal accounts in the same Northern banks that had made the original loans. Often it was both wasted and stolen.

Foolish loans

The experience was similar across the South. From the mid-1960s to the mid-1980s, despotism pervaded Latin America and employed an ingenious variety of scams wherever it went. In Asia and Africa, megalomaniacs with powerful friends and large appetites for personal wealth were financed with enthusiasm by the international banking fraternity. Indeed, it seemed to work so well that the credit lines became almost limitless – particularly if the governments in question were fighting on the 'right' side of the Cold War and buying large quantities of armaments from Northern suppliers.

Examples of these foolish loans to corrupt leaders are well known. In the Philippines, the dictator Ferdinand Marcos with his wife, Imelda, and their cronies are estimated to have pocketed in the form of kickbacks and commissions a third of all loans to that country. Before he was forced out of office, Marcos' personal wealth was estimated at $10 billion.

The Argentinean military dictatorship, famous for its 'dirty war' against so-called subversives, borrowed $40 billion from 1976 to 1983 and left no records for 80 per cent of the debt. Argentineans demanded that the Government either produce accounts or have the debts declared illegal. There is evidence that New York banks knew money was being misused, that there had been kickbacks and fraudulent loans to companies linked to the military, and that the IMF allegedly connived at the fraud. It is also clear that the military used some of the loans to buy weapons for the Falklands/Malvinas War. The crushing debt burden eventually led to the complete collapse of the Argentinean economy in late 2001. The country defaulted on nearly half its $180 billion repayment obligations the following year and there was tremendous popular pressure against taking on further foreign loans.

Deeper in debt
From 1997 to the first year of the millennium, the 'Jubilee 2000' citizens' movement led a worldwide campaign to cancel the debts of the world's poorest

countries. The campaign attracted millions of supporters, north and south. Jubilee researchers found
that almost a quarter of all Third World debt (nearly
$500 billion) is the result of loans used to prop up
dictators in some 25 different countries – sometimes
called 'odious debt'.[1] 'Odious', because citizens wonder
why they should be obliged to repay loans contracted
by corrupt governments who used the money to line
their own pockets.

The money flowed free and fast through the 1970s
and early 1980s. But eventually the soaring tower of
debt began to creak and sway. One government after
another began to run into financial trouble. The loans
they had raised and squandered on daft projects or
salted away in private bank accounts became so large
their foreign exchange earnings and tax revenues
couldn't keep up the payments.

During this period the IMF became an enforcer
of tough policy conditions on poor countries that
were forced to apply to it for temporary balance-of-
payments assistance. The IMF's loans were condi-
tional on governments following the advice of Fund
economists who had their own take on what Southern

PAYMENTS (in $ billions)
Total 1,607
160 160 163 172 191 230 262 269
90 — 91 — 92 — 93 — 94 — 95 — 96 — 97 year
132 133 154 175 172 229 252 292
RECEIPTS (in $ billions)
Total 1,530

**External debt: receipts and payments
(all developing countries) 1990-97
($ billions)**

World Development Report 1998/9, World Bank

South pays North

Most of the increase in
debt during the 1990s was
to pay interest on existing
loans. It was not used for
productive investment or
to tackle poverty. In six
of the eight years from
1990 to 1997, developing
countries paid out more
in debt service (interest
plus repayments) than they
received in new loans – a
total transfer from the poor
South to the rich North of
$77 billion. ∎

nations were doing wrong and how they could fix it. The Fund's demands were woven into the deals worked out with those countries that required an immediate transfusion of cash. Essentially, the agency argued that the debtor country's problems were caused by 'excessive demand' in the domestic economy. Curiously, the responsibility of the private banks that made most of the dubious loans in the first place (with their eyes wide open it should be noted) was ignored.

The IMF prescription

According to the Fund this excessive demand meant there were too many imports and not enough exports. The solution was to devalue the currency and cut government spending. This was supposed to slow the economy and reduce domestic demand, gradually resulting in fewer imports, along with more, and cheaper, exports. In time, the IMF argued, the balance-of-payments deficit would be eliminated. Countries were forced to adopt these austerity measures if they wanted to get the IMF 'seal of approval'. Without it they would be ostracized on the fringes of the global economy. As early as the 1970s both the IMF and the World Bank also urged debtor nations to take on deeper 'structural adjustment' measures but borrowing countries refused to go along with the advice.

Then in 1982 Mexico became the first indebted country to admit it could no longer meet its payments – a full-fledged Third World 'debt crisis' emerged. Northern politicians and bankers began to worry that the sheer volume of unpayable loans would undermine the world financial system. Widespread panic began to sweep through the world of international finance as scores of Southern nations teetered on the brink of economic collapse. In response both the Bank and the IMF hardened their line and began to demand major changes in the way debtor nations ran their domestic economies. Countries like Ghana were forced to impose tough adjustment conditions as early as 1983. A few years later, the US Treasury Secretary James Baker decided to formalize this new strategy to force Third World economies to radically 'restructure' their economies to meet their debt obligations. The 'Baker Plan' was introduced at the 1985 meeting of the World Bank and the IMF when both agencies were called on to impose more thorough 'adjustments' to the economic policies of debtor countries.

The Bank and the Fund made full use of this new leverage. Together they launched a policy to 'structurally adjust' the Third World by further deflating economies and demanding a withdrawal of government – not only from public enterprise but also from compassionate support of the basic health and welfare of the most vulnerable. Exports to earn foreign

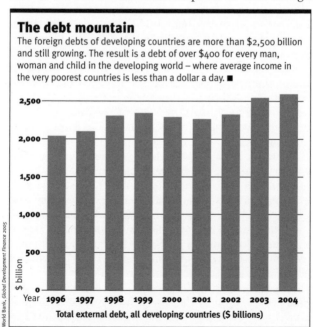

The debt mountain

The foreign debts of developing countries are more than $2,500 billion and still growing. The result is a debt of over $400 for every man, woman and child in the developing world – where average income in the very poorest countries is less than a dollar a day. ■

$ billion

Year — 1996, 1997, 1998, 1999, 2000, 2001, 2002, 2003, 2004

Total external debt, all developing countries ($ billions)

World Bank, Global Development Finance 2005

exchange were privileged over basic necessities, food production and other goods for domestic use.[2]

The Fund set up its first 'formal' Structural Adjustment Facility in 1986. The World Bank, cajoled by its more doctrinaire sibling, soon followed – by 1989 the Bank had contracted adjustment loans to 75 per cent of the countries that already had similar IMF loans in place. The Bank's conditions both extended and reinforced the IMF prescription for financial 'liberalization' and open markets. They included 'privatizing' state-owned enterprises; reducing the size and cost of government through massive public sector layoffs; cutting basic social services and subsidies on essential foodstuffs; and reducing barriers to trade. This restructuring was highly successful from the point of view of the private banks who siphoned off more than $178 billion from the South between 1984 and 1990 alone.[3] Structural-adjustment programs (SAPs) were an extremely effective mechanism for transforming private debt into public debt.

The 1980s were a 'lost decade' for much of the Third World. Growth stagnated and debt doubled to almost $1,500 billion by the decade's end. By 2002 it had reached nearly $2,500 billion. An ever-increasing proportion of this new debt was to service interest payments on the old debt, to keep money circulating and to keep the system up-and-running. Much of this debt had shifted from private banks to the IMF and the World Bank – even though the majority was still owed to rich country governments and Northern banks. The big difference was that the Fund and the Bank were always first in line so paying them was a much more serious prospect.

Taking more out
The stark fact that the Fund and the Bank began operating with reverse capital flows (in other words they were then taking more money out of the Third World

than they were putting back in) was sobering for those who believed those institutions were there to help.

In six of the eight years from 1990 to 1997 developing countries paid out more in debt service (interest plus repayments) than they received in new loans: a total transfer from South to North of $77 billion. Most of the increase was used to meet interest payments rather than for productive investment.[4] In 1998 the balance changed again as a result of massive bailout packages to Mexico and Asia. Nonetheless, recent figures for all private and public loans received by developing countries between 1998 and 2002 show that Southern nations repaid $217 billion more than they received in new loans over the same period.[5]

The 'conditionalities' of structural adjustment meanwhile diverted government revenues away from things like education and healthcare, towards debt repayment and the promotion of exports. This gave the World Bank and IMF a degree of control that even the most despotic of colonial regimes rarely achieved.

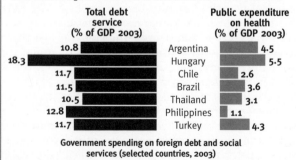

Creating poverty

In return for new loans to poor countries, lenders in the 1980s and 1990s insisted on 'structural adjustment' to increase their chances of being paid back. This meant cutting government spending on things like healthcare and education – the very services on which poor people (and women and children in particular) rely. Many of these countries have ended up spending more on servicing their debts than on the basic needs of their citizens. ∎

Total debt service (% of GDP 2003)		Public expenditure on health (% of GDP 2003)
10.8	Argentina	4.5
18.3	Hungary	5.5
11.7	Chile	2.6
11.5	Brazil	3.6
10.5	Thailand	3.1
12.8	Philippines	1.1
11.7	Turkey	4.3

Government spending on foreign debt and social services (selected countries, 2003)

Human Development Report 2005, UNDP

Even former 'economic shock-therapy' enforcers like Harvard University's Jeffrey Sachs were forced to reconsider their faith in this 'neo-liberal' recipe for economic progress. In 1999, Sachs wrote that many of the world's poorest people live in countries 'whose governments have long since gone bankrupt under the weight of past credits from foreign governments, banks and agencies such as the World Bank and the IMF. These countries have become desperate wards of the IMF... Their debts should be canceled outright and the IMF sent home.'[6]

The situation has remained essentially unchanged ever since. In nations as far apart as former Yugoslavia, Rwanda and Peru, the privations suffered in the name of debt repayments lay concealed behind outbreaks of violent civil unrest. All attempts to organize relief for the South were rebuffed on principle until 1996, when the 'Heavily Indebted Poor Countries Initiative' (HIPC) was launched to make debt repayments 'sustainable'. But the HIPC initiative has a checkered history. In 2003, the 27 countries receiving HIPC relief still spent $2.8 billion on debt repayments, between 15 and 20 per cent of government revenues. Most of those countries continued to spend more on debt service than on public health.[7] Within a decade, the 'Cold' war which ended in 1989 was replaced by a 'financial' war that is still being fought.

Two decades of structural adjustment has not only failed to solve the debt crisis, it has caused untold suffering for millions and led to widening gaps between rich and poor. A 1999 study by the Washington-based group, Development Gap, looked at the impact of SAPs on more than 70 African and Asian countries during the early 1990s. The study concluded that the longer a country operates under structural adjustment the worse its debt burden becomes. SAPs, Development Gap warned, 'are likely to push countries into a tragic circle of debt, adjustment, a weakened domestic economy, heightened vulnerability and greater debt.'[8]

Debt's legacy

So we are left with a bizarre and degrading spectacle. In Africa, external debt has ballooned by 400 per cent since the Bank and the IMF began managing national economies through structural adjustment. According to UN figures, Zambia has one of the highest rates of HIV/AIDS infection in the world, yet the southern African nation spends three times as much on debt service as it does on health. In Angola, where the average person lives to 40 years of age and 15 per cent of all babies die at birth, debt payments are nearly 5 times greater than spending on healthcare. In the late 1990s half of all primary-school age children in Africa were not in school yet governments spent four times more on debt payments than they spent on the health and education. Of course, debt is not the only issue here. Many poor nations mired in debt are also hobbled by venal politicians, widespread corruption and wasteful, bloated military budgets.

SAPs may not have put Third World countries back on a steady economic keel but they have certainly helped undermine democracy in those nations. Critics call it a new form of colonialism.

'Southern debt,' writes political scientist Susan George, 'has relatively little to do with money and finance, and everything to do with the West's continuing exercise of political and economic control. Just think of the advantages: no army, no costly colonial administration, rock-bottom prices for raw materials... It's a dream system and Western powers won't abandon it unless their own outraged citizens – or a far greater unity among debtor nations themselves – oblige them to so do.'[9]

Joseph Stiglitz, former World Bank Chief Economist, is candid about the record of bureaucrats in both agencies eroding the ability of states to govern their own affairs. In an article written shortly after his resignation Stiglitz said there are 'real risks associated with delegating excessive power to international agencies... The institution can actually become an interest group itself, concerned with maintaining its position and advancing its power.'[2]

Years later he continued his attack on the limitations of 'market fundamentalism' preached by the IMF and the World Bank. 'The institutions are dominated not just by the wealthiest industrial countries but by the commercial and financial interests in those countries and the policies naturally reflect this... The institutions are not representative of the nations they serve.'[10]

Servicing the national debt has become a major concern in rich and poor countries alike. But especially so in the South where there are far fewer dollars to spend: debt has become a major brake on development.

Dissenting voices

With the break-up of the Soviet Union, the booming economies of China and India and growing power of big corporations, the triumph of capitalism seems complete. Structural adjustment is an integral part of the system. Indeed, SAPs make sense when seen through the lens of an economic globalization which puts the economy ahead of people, rather than the other way round. This 'market fundamentalism' even has its own basic credo: the freedom of private corporations to trade, invest and move capital around the globe with a minimum amount of government interference.

But there are cracks emerging in this seemingly uniform consensus. People in the South are resisting structural adjustment through violent opposition and grassroots organizing. Protest too is coming from the millions uprooted by World Bank mega-projects, particularly the building of huge hydroelectric dams.

Debt and structural adjustment

Opposition to free trade is on the rise. And in Latin America, governments opposed to the 'Washington Consensus' have been elected in Uruguay, Argentina, Brazil, Bolivia, Venezuela and Chile. The one-size-fits-all model of economic globalization is no longer accepted. Religious extremism and the politics of ethnic exclusion (from Palestine to Iraq to India) are turning political costs into military ones. And, as continuing protests against the World Trade Organization and the G8 prove, powerful and unaccountable institutions are coming under pressure from citizens' groups, community activists, students, trade unionists and environmentalists. Many are calling for reform. Others are going much farther and demanding the outright abolition of these agencies and a complete restructuring of the global economic system.

1 'Take the hit!' by Joseph Hanlon, *New Internationalist*, No 312, May 1999. **2** *Economic Justice Report*, Ecumenical Coalition for Economic Justice, Vol X, No 4, December 1999. **3** 'How Bretton Woods re-ordered the world', *New Internationalist*, No 257, July 1994. **4** 'Debt: the facts', *New Internationalist*, No 312, May 1999. **5** *Your Money or Your Life*, Eric Toussaint, Haymarket, Chicago, 2005. **6** *The Independent*, London, 1 February 1999. **7** *Human Development Report 2005*, UNDP, New York, 2005. **8** 'Conditioning debt relief on adjustment: creating conditions for more indebtedness', Development Gap, Washington 1999. **9** *Another World Is Possible If...* , Susan George (Verso, London/New York, 2004). **10** *Globalization and its Discontents*, Joseph Stiglitz (Norton, New York/London, 2003).

4 The corporate century

Giant private companies have become the driving force behind economic globalization, wielding more power than many nation-states. Business values of 'efficiency' and 'competition' now dominate the debate on social policy, the public interest and the role of government. The tendency to monopoly, combined with decreasing rates of profit, drives and structures corporate decision-making – without regard for the social, environmental and economic consequences of those decisions.

ONE OF THE most jarring aspects of travel today is not the cultural differences – though thankfully those still exist – but the commercial similarities. Increasingly, where we travel to feels more and more like the place we just left.

Whether it's Montreal or Mumbai, Beijing or Buenos Aires, globalization has introduced a level of commercial culture which is eerily homogenous. The glitzy, air-conditioned shopping malls are interchangeable; the same shops sell the same goods. Fast food restaurants like KFC, Burger King and Taco Bell feature the same high-sugar, high-fat foods with minor concessions to local tastes. Young people use the same mobile phones, drink the same drinks, smoke the same cigarettes, wear identical branded clothing, play the same computer games, watch the same Hollywood films and listen to the same Western pop music.

Welcome to the world of the multinational corporation, a cultural and economic tsunami that is roaring across the globe and replacing the spectacular diversity of human society with a Westernized version of the good life. As corporations market the consumer dream of wealth and glamor, local cultures around the world are marginalized and devalued. Family and community bonds are disintegrating as social relationships are 'commodified' and reduced to what the English social critic Thomas Carlyle called the 'cash nexus' in his 1839 essay, *Chartism*. In the words of Swedish-born sociologist, Helena Norberg-Hodge, there is 'a global monoculture which is now able to disrupt traditional cultures with a shocking speed and finality and which surpasses anything the world has witnessed before.'[1]

Over the past two decades, as the global rules regulating the movement of goods and investment have been relaxed, private corporations have expanded their global reach so that their decisions now touch the lives of people in the most distant parts of the world. The vast, earth-straddling companies dominate global trade in everything from computers and pharmaceuticals to insurance, banking and cinema. Their holdings are so numerous and so Byzantine that it is often impossible to trace the chain of ownership. Even so it is estimated that a third of all trade in the international economy is between branches of the same corporation.

Some proponents of globalization argue that multinationals are the ambassadors of democracy. They insist that free markets and political freedoms are inextricably bound together and that the introduction of the first will inevitably lead to the second. Unfortunately, the facts don't support their claim. Market economies flourish in some of the world's most autocratic and tyrannical states and multinational corporations have shown surprisingly little interest in, and have had even less effect on, changing political systems. Saudi Arabia, Malaysia, Indonesia, Pakistan, China, Colombia: all have thriving market systems where multinational corporations are dominant actors. But they can scarcely be counted among the world's healthy democracies.

As the American political scientist Benjamin Barber has written: 'Capitalism requires consumers with access to markets and a stable political climate in order to succeed; such conditions may or may not be fostered by democracy, which can be disorderly and even anarchic in its early stages, and which often pursues public goods costly to or at odds with private market imperatives... capitalism does not need or entail democracy.'[2]

Many global corporations now wield more economic power than nation-states. When researchers at the Institute for Policy Studies in Washington last compiled figures in the year 2000, 51 of the largest 100 economies in the world were run by companies, not by countries. General Motors was bigger than Denmark; Wal-Mart was bigger than Poland, South Africa or

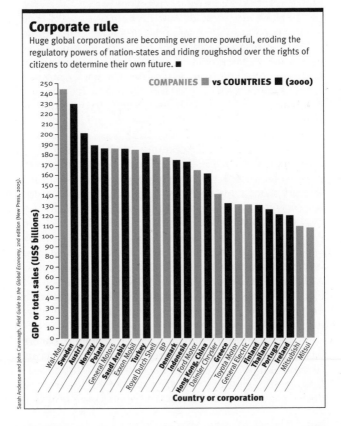

Corporate rule

Huge global corporations are becoming ever more powerful, eroding the regulatory powers of nation-states and riding roughshod over the rights of citizens to determine their own future. ■

COMPANIES ■ vs COUNTRIES ■ (2000)

GDP or total sales (US$ billions)

Country or corporation

Wal-Mart · Sweden · Austria · Norway · Poland · General Motors · Saudi Arabia · Exxon Mobil · Turkey · Royal Dutch Shell · BP · Denmark · Indonesia · Ford Motor · Hong Kong China · Daimler Chrysler · Greece · Toyota Motor · General Electric · Finland · Thailand · Portugal · Ireland · Mitsubishi · Mitsui

Sarah Anderson and John Cavanagh, *Field Guide to the Global Economy*, 2nd edition (New Press, 2005).

Greece; and Volkswagen was larger than Malaysia, Pakistan or Chile.[3]

The same study found:

- The world's top 200 corporations accounted for 25 per cent of global economic activity but employed less than one per cent of its workforce.
- Combined sales of the top 200 were 18 times more than the total annual income of 1.2 billion people living in absolute poverty – 24 per cent of the total world population.
- The profits of the top 200 grew 362.4 per cent from 1983 to 1999 while the number of people they employed grew by just 14.4 per cent.

Of course large companies have not just appeared on the scene. They've been with us since the early days of European expansion when governments routinely granted economic 'adventurers' like the Hudson Bay Company and the East India Company the right to control vast swaths of the planet in an attempt to consolidate imperial rule. But there has been nothing in history to match the economic muscle and political clout of today's giants – they grow larger and more powerful by the day. Scarcely a week goes by without another merger between major corporations. The global competition for market share over the past decade has been the catalyst for the biggest shift towards monopoly in the last century.

In 2000 the world's biggest internet provider, America Online (AOL), announced a $160-billion merger with Time-Warner. The UK-based music giant EMI then unveiled plans for a $20 billion liaison with Time-Warner – creating the world's largest music firm. Other recent mergers include the purchase of Chrysler Motors by the German company Daimler-Benz for $43 billion; the $1.75 billion purchase of iconic computer giant IBM's personal computer division by the Chinese company, Lenovo; and the $1.5 billion takeover of Canada's Hudson's Bay Company (originally incorporated in 1670) by US leveraged buy-out specialist Jerry Zucker. Meanwhile, in Europe the governments of both France and Luxembourg opposed the $26 billion hostile takeover of Arcelor SA by the world's biggest steel company, India-based Mittal. The merger would create the world's first 100-million-ton-plus steel producer, with a market capitalization of $45 billion.

UN figures indicated the tendency towards monopoly is growing across a range of industries, including manufacturing, banking and finance, media and entertainment, and communication technologies. But high-profile business marriages are also taking place in older industries like automobiles and transport as well as in primary resources such as mining, forestry and agriculture. The 10 largest corporations in their field now control 86 per cent of the telecommunications sector, 85 per cent of the pesticides industry, 70 per cent of the computer industry and 35 per cent of the pharmaceutical industry.

According to the accounting firm KPMG, the global mergers and acquisition market in 2005 involved 24,806 deals worth a combined $2,059 billion, a 19 per cent leap over the previous year. Stock markets reward the merged corporations with higher share prices on the grounds that the new larger firms will be more 'efficient' and therefore increase company earnings. But what does that notion of 'efficiency' really mean? Mergers squander vast amounts of resources for no productive purpose. The public impact of this very private decision-making process is rarely considered. When two corporate giants merge it inevitably leads to thousands of job losses and scores of factory closings. In fact this is precisely the point – to bolster the bottom line by trimming costs. For example when the UK companies Glaxo (now GlaxoSmithKline) and Wellcome merged in early 1999 a tenth of the total workforce (7,500 workers) lost their jobs. Good news for shareholders, but not so good news if you were one of the workers who received your dismissal notice.

Merging businesses

Business executives champion the economic 'common sense' of mergers and push for their approval on the grounds that getting bigger is the only way to compete in a lean-and-mean global marketplace. But while size does matter in terms of a company's ability to compete, ironically a smaller number of large companies also heightens the tendency towards monopoly by eliminating competition. The easiest way to get rid of a competitor is to buy them out. Giant companies also have greater powers to wrest concessions from national and regional governments simply because they are such dominant economic players, creating jobs (albeit fewer of them) and boosting national income.

The spate of mergers and acquisitions (M&As) over the last decade reflects the quickly changing nature of the global economy, especially the loosening of foreign investment regulations and the liberalization of international capital flows. Companies are

Engulf and Devour, Inc.

Globalization has sparked a frenzy of corporate mergers and acquisitions (M&As). These mega-companies threaten competition and increase the threat of monopoly.

In 2005 over $2,059 billion was spent on corporate M&As. The biggest deals were in telecommunications, finance, oil and gas, and retail. ∎

Big deals

Buyer	Nationality	Target	Price ($US billion)
Procter & Gamble	US	Gillette	$60.7
Mitsubishi Financial	Japan	UFJ Holdings	$59.1
Sprint Corp	US	Nextel	$45.2
Telecom Italia	Italy	Telecom Italia Mobile	$27.9
SBC Communications	US	AT&T	$23.9
Chevron Texaco	US	Unocal	$18.9
Pernod Ricard	France	Allied Domecq	$17.8
Federated Dept Stores	US	May Dept Stores	$17.6

'Global upturn in M&As fuelled by Asia', 12/12/05, KPMG International, www.kpmg.com

now freer to compete globally, to grow and expand into overseas markets – and the recent shift to free trade in goods, services and investment capital is furthering this consolidation.

The assumption that competition is good 'in and of itself' is central to the corporate-led model of economic globalization. It's this belief that has led to a worldwide campaign by the economically powerful in favor of privatizing publicly-owned enterprises. According to this conservative view, government must be downsized and its role in the provision of public services curtailed. The argument is that governments are inefficient, bloated bureaucracies that waste taxpayers' money – so they must be restrained. This criticism resonates to some extent with most people, left and right, on the political spectrum. Perhaps that's why when right-wing critics began to bemoan the costs of big government in the 1970s it didn't take them long to find a sympathetic ear. But rather than strengthen the role of the State by streamlining bureaucratic inefficiencies and making government work better, they argued that private business should do the job instead.

This manic enthusiasm for privatization exploded when Margaret Thatcher came to power in Britain in 1979. State-owned enterprises were sold off: the national airline, government-run water, gas, telephone and electric utilities, and the railway system. From 1979 to 1994 the overall number of jobs in the public sector in the UK was reduced from seven million to five million. During the same period the number of new jobs created by the private sector was minimal and the bulk of those jobs were in the non-unionized, low-paid, service sector. In the case of British Rail, the 1996 privatization created an inefficient, accident-prone system supported by massive public subsidies. In 2001 the number of cancellations reached 165,000 – nearly three times the level of 1999. More than 2,000 contractors were involved in maintaining infrastructure.[4] For a one-off payment to the public purse the UK Government sold state-owned enterprises that had contributed guaranteed, yearly profits to the Treasury.

While much was made of the opportunity for ordinary British people to buy shares in the newly-privatized public utilities, the reality was quite different. Nine million UK residents did buy shares but most of them invested less than £1,000 and sold them quickly when they found they could turn a quick profit.

The majority of shares of the former publicly-owned companies are now controlled by institutional investors and wealthy individuals. Susan George has called privatization, 'the alienation and surrender of the product of decades of work by thousands of people to a tiny minority of large investors'.[5]

As governments adopt the private enterprise model and cut public expenditure they open up areas to market forces that were previously considered the responsibility of the state. After World War Two, politicians in the West were forced by a civic-minded electorate to expand social welfare policies including education, healthcare, unemployment insurance, state pensions and other social security measures. At the same time the state expanded its role in the provision of public infrastructure, building roads, bridges, dams, airports, prisons and hospitals.

Now, with the notion of the 'inefficient' public sector firmly fixed in people's minds, governments are selling off public utilities like water, electricity and airports – often because operating budgets have been slashed to ribbons. Even prisons and parks are being privatized as governments pare public expenditure to meet market demands for balanced budgets. Make no mistake about it, these areas offer tremendous scope for profits. In the US alone the total budget for prisons and jails in 1997 was more than $31 billion.

Privatizing healthcare

Other areas are also being eyed enthusiastically by the profit-making sector. State-funded healthcare is a case in point. In Canada, Britain, Australia and Europe private companies are making major inroads into publicly-financed healthcare as deficit-conscious politicians slash budgets. At the international level, the General Agreement on Trade in Services (GATS), administered by the World Trade Organization (WTO) was created in 1994. One of the goals of the GATS is to classify the public health sector as part of the 'service industry', eventually opening the door to full-scale commercialization along the lines of the American model where private corporations are dominant.

The for-profit health sector in the US has been actively lobbying to pave the way for their overseas expansion. A document by the US Coalition of Service Industries in November 1999 suggested that Washington push the WTO to 'encourage more privatization' and to provide 'market access and national treatment allowing provision of all healthcare services cross-border'. The ultimate goal was clearly spelled out: to allow 'majority foreign ownership of healthcare facilities'. The dry, technical language of the market is already infecting the debate around healthcare policy. But the great fear for those defending universal, state-funded healthcare is that privatization will lead to a two-tier system where wealthy patients pay for quick, high-tech care while the rest of us put up with poorly equipped, under-funded hospitals, long waiting lists and overworked doctors, nurses and technicians.

Privatization has been strongly endorsed by both the World Bank and the IMF and is a standard ingredient in any 'structural adjustment' prescription. It is based on the notion that governments really have no business in the marketplace and that the least government is the best government. Despite the convincing claims of its critics the Bank remains wedded to privatization.

Its Private Sector Development Strategy released in February 2002 reinforces what it calls 'policy-based lending to promote privatization'. The initiative seeks to expand the Bank's business-friendly division, the International Finance Corporation, whose role is to open doors for private companies, both foreign and domestic. The emphasis is on increasing the role of private business in the service sector: water, sanitation, electricity, education and healthcare.

How much negotiating room do poor nations have to reject or shape adjustment policies which are presented to them by the Bank or the IMF as conditions of borrowing? The answer is virtually none. The right of governments (elected or otherwise) to make sovereign policy decisions on behalf of their citizens – a basic tenet of democracy – is jettisoned. The Bank and the IMF have been enforcing market fundamentalism for decades. Often privatization is a 'condition' for release of aid funds. To qualify for debt relief under the Bank's Heavily Indebted Poor Countries Initiative (HIPC) Southern nations are instructed to fall into line. According to an Oxfam-UK report, debt relief to Honduras under an HIPC agreement was delayed for six months when the IMF demanded more progress on electricity privatization.[6]

Largely due to this arm-twisting the sale of state assets has swept across the developing world and the former Soviet Union. In Russia, the transition to private ownership was riddled with corruption. Former Communist Party *apparatchiks* wound up in control of most state assets while billions hemorrhaged out of the country into numbered Swiss bank accounts. According to business writer Paul Klebnikov the country suffered its worst economic decline since the Nazi invasion of 1942: 'There was a 42-per-cent decline in GDP. The population was impoverished. Mortality rates rocketed and the Russian State was essentially bankrupt.'[7]

Privatization in the South has been bedeviled by corruption, regulatory failure and corporate bullying. Take the energy sector. Often companies are reluctant to invest in power projects without a guaranteed return. Enter the 'power-purchase agreement' – a legal sleight-of-hand which requires a publicly owned electricity distributor to buy power from private producers at a fixed price in US dollars for up to 30 years – even if demand swoons and the power is not used. In India, the Maharashtra State Electricity Board (MSEB) was taken to the cleaners by the now-disgraced Enron Corporation and its $920-million Dabhol power plant. At one point, after renegotiating the power purchase deal, the MSEB was obliged to pay Enron $30 billion a year. Indian critics called the deal 'the most massive fraud in the country's history'. Indian novelist and activist Arundhati Roy says that the MSEB was forced to cut production from its own plants to buy power from Dabhol and hundreds of small industries had to close because they couldn't afford the expensive power. 'Privatization,' Roy writes, 'is presented as being the only alternative to an inefficient, corrupt state. In fact, it's not a choice at all... [it's a] mutually profitable business contract between the private company (preferably foreign) and the ruling élite of the Third World.'[8]

Attracting the money

In addition to selling off public assets, governments are constantly looking to attract private foreign investment. But investment by foreign corporations is by no means a guarantee of economic progress.

For example a large part of foreign direct investment (FDI) is made up of companies buying out state firms, purchasing equity in local companies or financing mergers and acquisitions. Cross-border M&As account for about 80 per cent of total foreign direct investment yearly. Little of this ends up in new productive activity and there is almost always a net loss of jobs as a result of downsizing after mergers are completed. Increased investment from abroad can also cause a net drain on foreign exchange as multinational companies remit profits to their overseas headquarters. If a foreign corporation produces mainly for local markets, and especially if it edges out local suppliers rather than replacing imports, it may significantly worsen balance of payments problems.

Controlling foreign investment

It's not the quantity of FDI that matters but the quality. National governments need to select the kinds of foreign investment that will produce net benefits for their citizens and reject those investments whose overall impact will be negative. Foreign investment can make a positive contribution to national development but only if it is channeled into productive rather than speculative activities. Unfortunately, the ability to shape foreign investment is dwindling as free-trade arrangements and bilateral trade agreements effectively tie the hands of states which agree to them, inevitably compromising government sovereignty.

Nonetheless, most Southern governments are anxious to attract investment from multinationals – despite the concern about corporate power and unethical behavior. With good reason – global companies are extremely skilled at delivering the goods. They are at the cutting edge of technological innovation and they can introduce new management and marketing strategies. And it's generally the case that wages and working conditions are usually better in foreign subsidiaries than in local companies.

But overseas investors don't automatically favor countries simply because they've loosened regulations on profit remittances or corporate taxes. The big money predictably goes to where it's safest and where the potential for profit is greatest. Most direct investment is concentrated in a small number of developing countries. According to UNCTAD's 2005 *World Investment Report*, more than two-thirds of all FDI to the South and the ex-Soviet bloc went to just 10 countries and the bulk went to just one country – China.

Multinationals are also major players in research and development (R&D). They account for close to half of global R&D expenditures and that spending can eclipse that of many countries. Ford, Pfizer, DaimlerChrysler, Siemens, Toyota and General Motors spent more than $5 billion on R&D in 2003. In the South, only Brazil, China, South Korea and Taiwan spent more. The world's largest R&D spenders are concentrated in a few industries – IT hardware, the automotive industry, pharmaceuticals and biotechnology.

Draining the public purse

Investors crave stability which is why nearly 60 per cent of all foreign investment goes to industrial countries. The US, UK, Luxembourg, Australia, Belgium, France and Spain received the lion's share in 2004. Yet even in the West corporations have the upper hand, trading off one nation against another to see who can offer the most lucrative investment incentives. Governments drain the public purse in their attempts to buy jobs from private investors. Tax holidays, interest-free loans, research grants, training schemes, unhindered profit remittances and publicly-funded sewers, roads and utilities are among the mix of 'incentives' that companies now expect in return for opening up a new factory or office.

The largest multinationals call themselves 'global firms' which might lead one to believe that they are stateless, disembodied entities toiling for the good of humankind. The truth is more complex. There are few giant companies that are truly stateless; most are firmly tied to one national home base. Microsoft and Ford Motor Company are identifiably US corporations, Total is French, Siemens is German, Vodafone is British and News Corporation is Australian. These companies have no problem wrapping themselves in the national flag when it comes to lobbying local governments for tax breaks, start-up grants or other goodies. But at the same time their allegiances are fickle – and quickly diverted if opportunities for profit appear greater elsewhere. The fact that multinational corporations are relatively footloose means they can move operations to where costs are cheapest – and play off one government against another in the process. Examples fill the business press daily. In September 2005 Bombardier, a Canadian company which had received millions in government subsidies, announced it was exporting 500 highly-paid, skilled jobs to India, China and Mexico, claiming it needed to 'return to profitability by reducing operating costs'.[9] This political power – to pull up stakes, lay off workers and shift production elsewhere – is a powerful bargaining chip which business can use to wrest greater concessions from job-hungry governments.

One of the corporate sector's greatest political victories in recent decades has been to beat down corporate taxes. In Britain, the corporate tax rate fell from 52 per cent in 1979 to 30 per cent in 2000 and Labor Prime Minister Tony Blair has boasted that British business is subject to fewer strictures than corporations in the US. Corporate tax rates have declined in virtually every OECD country over the last two decades as governments rely more and more on personal income taxes and sales taxes for revenues. In 1950 corporate taxes in the US accounted for 30 per cent of government funds; today they account for less than 12 per cent. In Canada, the effective corporate tax rate was cut from 28 per cent to 21 per cent from 2000 to 2004 while corporate profits as a share of national income hit an all time high.

Their sheer size, wealth and power means that multinationals and the business sector in general have been able to structure the public debate on social issues and the role of government in a way that benefits their own interests. They have used their louder voices and political clout to build an effective propaganda machine and to boost what the great Italian political theorist Antonio Gramsci called their 'cultural hegemony'. Through sophisticated public relations, media manipulation and friends-in-high-places the orthodoxy of corporate-led globalization has become the 'common sense' approach to running a country. This radical paradigm shift has occurred in the short space of 40 years – an extraordinary accomplishment by a cadre of right-wing think tanks, radical entrepreneurs and their academic supporters.

The more our lives become entangled in the market the more the ideology of profit before people becomes accepted. A corporation's ultimate responsibility is to not to society but to its shareholders, as Chief Executive Officers (CEOs) constantly reassure their investors at annual general meetings. Enhanced value for shareholders drives and structures corporate decision-making – without regard for the social, environmental and economic consequences of those decisions. The public is the loser. Unless social obligations are imposed on companies the business agenda will continue to ride roughshod over national and community interests.

NAFTA was one of the first regional economic pacts developed to further corporate globalization. The Washington-based, non-governmental organization, Public Citizen, has documented a steady movement of American companies to cheap labor zones in Mexico and the direct loss of hundreds of thousands of jobs since NAFTA came into effect in 1995.

The activist group cites the example of the jeans maker Guess? Inc. which, according to the *Wall Street Journal*, cut the percentage of its clothes sewn in Los Angeles from 97 per cent prior to NAFTA to 35 per cent two years later. In that period the company relocated five sewing factories to Mexico and others to Peru and Chile. More than 1,000 workers in Los Angeles lost their jobs. At the same time Public Citizen notes that corporate supporters of the trade deal can't provide documentation for more than a few thousand NAFTA job gains. According to the Washington-based Economic Policy Institute, the deal eliminated nearly 880,000 jobs. Most jobs lost to NAFTA were in high-paying manufacturing, the ones that replaced them were in the low-paid, non-unionized service sector. NAFTA also had a negative effect on the wages of US workers whose jobs have not been relocated. They are now in direct competition with skilled, educated Mexican workers who work for a dollar or two an hour – or less. As a result their bargaining power with their employers has been substantially lessened. NAFTA was supposed to solve this problem by raising Mexican living standards and wages. Instead, both have plummeted, harming the economic prospects for workers on both sides of the border.

NAFTA's labor side-agreement was supposed to cushion workers but it didn't work out that way. Instead, labor protections built into Mexico's legal system have been attacked as obstacles to investment. In 2002, Mexican President Vicente Fox announced he would support the World Bank's recommendations to scrap most of Mexico's Federal Labor Law – eliminating mandatory severance pay and the 40-hour week. Mexico's historic (though not always enforced) ban on strike-breaking and guarantees of healthcare and housing would be gutted as well.

The policy of encouraging foreign investment at all cost also led to the wholesale privatization of Mexican industry over the past decade and the effects have been devastating. While three-quarters of the workforce belonged to unions three decades ago, less than 30 per cent does today. Private owners reduced the membership of the railway workers' union from 90,000 to 36,000.

During the last two decades the income of Mexican workers has lost 76 per cent of its purchasing power. Under pressure from foreign lenders, the Mexican Government ended subsidies on the prices of basic necessities – including gasoline, electricity, bus fares, tortillas and milk – all of which have risen drastically. An estimated 40 million people live in poverty and 25 million in extreme poverty. The country's new independent union federation, the National Union of Workers, claims more than nine million people are out of work – a quarter of the workforce.

Well before NAFTA the disparity between US and Mexican wages was growing. Mexican salaries were a third of those in the US in the 1970s. They are now less than an eighth. It is this disparity which both impoverishes Mexican workers and acts as a magnet drawing production from the US. By exacerbating these trends NAFTA forced working communities in Canada, the US and Mexico to ask some basic questions.[10]

The upper hand

As corporations gain the upper hand, fear of job losses and the resulting social devastation has created a downward pressure on environmental standards and social programs – what critics of unregulated corporate power call 'a race to the bottom'.

Mexico after 10 years of NAFTA (North American Free Trade Agreement)

Exports increased 300% from 1993-2002 to $161 million. But...
• Annual GDP growth has been less than 1%.
• More than half of manufactured exports have been from the oil industry or from low-wage maquiladora assembly plants along the US border.
• Of the 6 biggest export firms, 5 are foreign-owned and account for more than 20% of total exports.

Treaties like NAFTA, and new trade rules backed by the WTO, empower corporations while restricting national governments from interfering with the 'wisdom' of the market. But business is constantly pushing to expand the freedom to trade and invest, unhindered by either government regulations or social obligations.

The Multilateral Agreement on Investment (MAI) was one infamous example of the attempt by big business to remake the world in its image.

Public disillusionment with the WTO is well known. But if activists hadn't stumbled across the MAI in 1997, efforts to inject human values into the debate on the global trading system could have been severely curtailed. After the WTO was created in 1994, the globe's major corporations began to put together a plan for codifying the rules of world trade in a way that would give them complete freedom. They found it in the MAI, an agreement which was drafted by the International Chamber of Commerce (a 'professional association' of the world's largest companies) and presented to the rich-nation OECD members for discussion and, it was assumed, rubber-stamp approval.

Third World governments were rightly suspicious of the MAI and many saw it as 'a throwback to colonial era economics'. But, with the weight of the OECD behind it, supporters of the MAI reckoned it would be speedily adopted as an official WTO document.

Delegates from OECD countries began discussing the MAI in early 1995 behind closed doors. By early 1997 most of the treaty was down on paper and the public was none the wiser. In fact, most politicians in the OECD's 29 member countries weren't even aware of the negotiations. When activists in Canada got their hands on a copy of the MAI and began sending it around the world via the internet the full scope of the document became clear.

Essentially the agreement set out to give private companies the same legal status as nation-states in all countries that were party to the Agreement. But more importantly it laid out a clear set of rules so that corporations would be able to defend their new rights against the objections of sovereign governments. The MAI was so overwhelmingly biased towards the interests of multinationals that critics were quick to label it 'the corporate rule treaty'.

MAI protest

For example, under MAI provisions corporations could sue governments for passing laws that might reduce their potential profits. They could make their case in secret with no outside interest groups involved and the decision would be binding. The MAI also allowed foreign investors to challenge public funding of social programs as a distortion of free markets and the 'level playing field'. If a government chose to privatize a state-owned industry it could no longer give preference to domestic buyers. In addition, governments would be forbidden to demand that foreign investment benefit local communities or the national economy. They could not demand domestic content, local hiring, affirmative action, technology transfer or anything else in return for allowing foreign companies to exploit publicly owned resources. And there were to be no limits on profit repatriation.

Once the text became public, citizens' groups around the world began vigorous education campaigns on the potentially-damaging impact of the MAI. Two influential activists, Tony Clarke and Maude Barlow, summed up the feelings of citizens' groups everywhere. 'The MAI', they wrote, 'would provide foreign investors with new and substantive rights with which they could challenge government programs, policies and laws all over the world.'[11]

In a few months public anxiety about the deal came to a head. In France, Australia, Canada and the US politicians at all levels were drawn into the debate and governments were forced to enter 'reservations' to protect themselves from certain of the MAI's provisions. By the May 1998 deadline it was clear that the talks were at a standstill and that public opposition had torpedoed further progress on the Agreement.

This was a stunning victory for a growing international citizens' movement. But the end of the MAI as such did not spell the end of the corporate agenda for a global investment treaty. The focus would now shift to the WTO and other venues where multinationals could lobby for the MAI-like investment provisions.

The downward pressure on wages and social programs caused by economic globalization is compounded by the rise of free trade zones (FTZs) which exist in dozens of Third World countries – there are now more than 1,000 FTZs operating from Malaysia and the Philippines to El Salvador, Mexico and even

---

Korten on corporations
Critic and author **David Korten** reflects on corporate power.

Corporations say the solution to poverty is to stimulate growth and create more wealth for everyone. Do you think that approach will work?
There is little evidence that economic growth alleviates poverty. Since 1950 the world's total economic output has increased five-fold while the number of people living in absolute poverty has doubled. This growth has pushed human demands on the eco-system beyond what the planet is capable of sustaining. And that does two things: it accelerates the rate of breakdown of the planet's ability to regenerate its natural systems. And it intensifies the competition between rich and poor for the resources that remain. I now believe that what the Gross National Product (GNP) really measures is the rate at which the economically powerful are expropriating the resources of the economically weak in order to convert them into products that quickly become the garbage of the rich.
Corporate leaders and their government backers claim free trade and open markets are the only way to have an efficient market system. Does business know best?
The modern corporation is specifically designed to concentrate economic power, and to protect the people who use that power from liability for the consequences of its uses. Free-trade agreements like NAFTA and GATT are not really trade agreements at all. They are

socialist Cuba. These officially sanctioned sites exist almost as separate countries, offering their corporate clients minimal taxes, lax environmental regulations, cheap labor and low overheads.

Overcapacity

In their urgent effort to grow, corporations have ignored a fundamental aspect of capitalist production: over-capacity. It was Henry Ford, one of the pioneers of mass production, who realized 80 years ago the inherent dilemma of replacing labor with machines and then paying the remaining workers poverty-level wages. You could produce a lot of cars but in the end you would have no-one who could afford to buy them: too many goods and too few buyers. Today, sophisticated improvements in manufacturing equipment have boosted productivity while destroying millions of jobs

economic integration agreements intended to guarantee the rights of global corporations to move both goods and investments wherever they wish – free from public interference or accountability. Corporate power really lies in this ability to manipulate communities and markets in their own interest.

As corporations replace workers with technology they gain even more clout. Local governments are now forced not only to give them tax breaks but to subsidize directly their operations as well. This is what global competition is really about – communities and workers competing against each other to absorb even more of the production costs of the world's most powerful and profitable companies.

Is sustainable growth possible?

In my view 'green growth' is an oxymoron. In a deregulated market economy global corporations are accountable to only one master, a rogue financial system with one incessant demand – keep your stock price as high as possible by maximizing short-term returns. One way to do that is to shift as much of the cost of the corporation's operations as possible onto the community. The goal is to externalize costs and privatize gain.

A green corporation simply can't last in our unregulated market economy where competing companies are not internalizing their costs. If you do attempt to 'green' your business you'll soon be bought out by some corporate raiders who see an opportunity to externalize costs and make a short-term killing. ■

Adapted from 'Development is a sham', *NI 278*, April 1996.

and curbing wage growth. Henry Ford's own automobile sector is a case in point. One of the major reasons for the massive restructuring in that industry over the past decade is over-capacity, which is estimated at more than 25 to 30 per cent worldwide. According to *The Economist* the global auto industry can produce 20 million more vehicles a year than the market can absorb. And soon low-cost Chinese auto makers will be joining the fray. Knowledgeable observers predict there will be just half a dozen major auto companies within a decade.

There is a global over-capacity in everything from shoes and steel to clothing and electronic goods. One estimate puts the excess manufacturing capacity in China at more than 40 per cent. As industries consolidate to cut losses, factories are closed but output remains the same or even increases. This produces falling rates of profit which in turn drives industry to look for further efficiencies. One tack is to continue to cut labor costs – which helps the bottom line initially but actually dampens global demand over time. Another is the merger and acquisition route – cut costs by consolidating production, closing factories and laying off workers. However, this too is self-defeating in the long run since it also inevitably reduces demand.

The real danger of this overproduction is 'deflation'. Instead of a steady rise in employment and relatively stable prices for commodities and manufactured goods, deflation is a downward spiral of both prices and wages. In economic terms the logic is simple: productive capacity exceeds demand, prices fall, unemployment rises and wages are forced down farther.

In the 1930s the result was a resounding and destructive economic crash which saw plants close and millions of workers made redundant. This catastrophe was reversed only when factories boosted production of armaments and other supplies for the Second World War. So far the specter of deflation has been kept at bay by making the US economy the 'consumer of last resort'. According to the IMF, the US has provided about half the growth in total world demand since 1988. Fueled by a strong dollar and a vastly over-valued stock market, the American economy continues to suck in cheap imports from the rest of the world. Every day Americans borrow three billion dollars from foreigners – a form of 'vendor financing' – to pay for imports and to keep domestic interest rates low. The result is colossal domestic debt and record trade deficits. In 2005, the US trade deficit soared to $726 billion – more than twice the deficit of six years earlier. China's trade surplus with the United States increased by 24.5 per cent in 2005, to a whopping $202 billion, the country's largest bilateral deficit.

Fight for prosperity

In an era of globalized free markets all countries try to fight their way to prosperity by boosting exports. That's partly because traditional Keynesian methods of stimulating domestic growth by 'priming the pump' have fallen into disfavor and few countries now have either the inclination or the political will to direct domestic savings toward investment in the local mar-ket. Instead, all nations look outwards, depending on international trade for their economic survival. This focus on trade is reflected in the data. According to the WTO, the value of world merchandise trade rose by 21 per cent in 2004 to $8.88 trillion while world services trade jumped by 16 per cent to $2.10 trillion. Yet, as UNDP's 2005 *Human Development Report* points out: 'After more than two decades of rapid trade growth, high-income countries representing 15 per cent of the world's population still account for two-thirds of world exports – a modest decline from the position in 1980.'

The success of any country vis-à-vis another depends on how competitively (ie how cheaply) it can price its goods in the world market. This kind of competition inevitably means cutting costs and the easiest costs to cut are wages. But as we have already seen, cheap labor exports inevitably backfire by undermining domestic purchasing power and depressing domestic demand. Simply put: workers earn less so they have less to spend. As University of Ottawa economist Michel Chossudovsky notes: 'the expansion of exports from developing countries is predicated on the contraction of internal purchasing power. Poverty is an input on the supply side.'[12]

Over the past 15 years the UN has documented a steady shift of global income from wages to profits. Even so investors are no longer satisfied with 5 or 6 per cent annual returns. Trade and investment barriers started to crumble as economic globalization took hold. But corporations, banks and other major investors were looking for quicker ways of maximizing their returns. The solution was at hand. From the 'real' economy of manufacturing and commodity production investors turned to the world of international finance. Speculation and gambling in international money markets seemed easier than competing for fewer and fewer paying customers in the old goods and services economy. Welcome to the era of the 'global casino'.

1 'The march of the monoculture', Helena Norberg-Hodge, *The Ecologist*, Vol 29, No 2, May/June 1999. 2 *Jihad vs McWorld*, Benjamin R Barber (Ballantine Books, New York, 1995). 3 *Top 200: The Rise of Corporate Global Power*, Sarah Anderson and Jon Cavanagh (Institute for Policy Studies, Washington, 2000). 4 'Derailed', Brendan Martin, *Multinational Monitor*, Jan/Feb 2002. 5 'A short history of neo-liberalism', Susan George, paper presented to the conference on Economic sovereignty in a globalizing world, Bangkok, March 1999. 6 'Privatization and poverty', K Bayliss, Jan 2002, http://idpm.man.ac.uk/crc/. 7 'The theft of the century', *Multinational Monitor*, Jan/Feb 2002. 8 *Power politics*, Arundhati Roy (South End Press, Boston, 2001). 9 '90 more Downsview plan jobs may flee', *The Toronto Star*, p C5, 27 September 2005. 10 Excerpted from 'Up for grabs', David Bacon, *New Internationalist*, No374 December 2004. 11 This description of the battle against the MAI owes much to MAI Round 2: new global and internal threats to Canadian sovereignty, Tony Clarke and Maude Barlow (Stoddart, 1998). 12 *The globalization of poverty*, Michel Chossudovsky (Third World Network, 1997).

5 Global casino

The deregulation of global finance coupled with the microelectronics revolution has sparked a surge in the international flow of capital. This uncontrolled speculation has eclipsed long-term productive investment and poses a huge threat to the stability of the global economy. Recent financial crises caused suffering for millions and confirm the need for urgent action to control the money markets and rein in currency traders.

THE ACCELERATION OF economic globalization is dramatically altering life for people around the world. As wealth increases for a minority of humankind, disparities between rich and poor widen and the assault on our planet's natural resources speeds up.

But the biggest and most dangerous change over the past 35 years has been in the area of global finance. The volume of worldwide foreign exchange transactions has exploded as country after country has lowered barriers to foreign investment. In 1980 the daily average of foreign exchange trading totaled $80 billion. Today it is estimated that more than $1.9 trillion changes hands every day on global currency markets. That is about 50 times greater than the total value of all goods and services traded globally each year. An unimaginable sum of money.[1] But it is all the more stunning when you realize that most of this investment has virtually nothing to do with producing real goods or services for real people.

The world of international finance is technically arcane but the main point is easily understood. The goal is to make money – the end-use of the investment is relevant only to the extent that it is profitable. As growth in the real economy declines due to over-capacity and shrinking wages worldwide, speculative investment has grown. Money chasing money has eclipsed productive investment as the engine of the global economy.

There are very few controls on the movement of international capital. Yet the predominant view of the Bretton Woods institutions, the giant global banks and private corporations is that the world needs more financial liberalization, not less.

Others are not so sure. They're more inclined to believe what Keynes wrote in his 1936 book *The General Theory of Employment, Interest and Money*. 'Speculators may do no harm as bubbles on a steady stream of enterprise,' he warned, 'but the position is serious when enterprise becomes the bubble on a whirlpool of speculation.'

The rules for running the global economy, laid down at Bretton Woods after World War Two, specifically sought to rein in finance capital and contain it within national borders. Keynes was Britain's delegate to the meeting. He warned that unregulated flows of international capital would remove power from elected politicians and put it into the hands of the rich investors – whose ultimate allegiance was to their own self-interest.

Today that self-interest is creating havoc. Since governments in the industrialized countries began to deregulate financial markets in 1979, short-term speculation has become the single-largest component in the flow of international investment. Managers of billion-dollar hedge funds, mutual funds and pension plans move money in and out of countries at lightning speed based on fractional differences in exchange rates. This volatile flow of currency is almost completely detached from the physical economy. For every dollar that is needed to facilitate the trade in real goods, nine dollars is gambled in foreign exchange markets.

Critics of corporate-led globalization charge that unregulated flows of capital pose a major threat to the stability of the world economy, turning it into a 'global

Riding the whirlpool

More than $1.9 trillion ($1,900 billion) changes hands daily on global currency markets.

- The *annual* global trade in merchandise and services in 2004 was $10.98 billion. Given that exchange markets have about 200 working days, this is the equivalent of just 1.15 days of trading on foreign exchange (forex) markets.

- An estimated 95% of all forex deals are short-term speculation; more than 80% are completed in less than a week and 40% in less than two days.

- From 1986 to 2004 the volume of forex transactions increased ten-fold, from just under $200 billion to $1,900 billion. ∎

Rate of growth of foreign exchange markets

Figures for daily turnover in foreign exchange trading

Billions of dollars

1986 1989 1992 1995 1998 2001 2004

The Global Gamblers, British Banks and the Foreign Exchange Game, War on Want, 1999. 2004 Triennial Central Bank Survey of Foreign Exchange and Derivatives Market Activity, Bank for International Settlements, www.bis.org

financial casino'. This free flow of capital has also had a direct political impact, leaving national governments hostage to market forces. Any departure from the received wisdom is instantly punished. Without regulation investors can pull up stakes at a moment's notice. Governments are hesitant to introduce laws that might upset investors and cause capital to flee, possibly sparking economic chaos. This threat leads to a massive degree of self-censorship and reduces the political space for governments to control their own economic destiny. Such is the power of finance capital.

Currency speculation

The development of sophisticated computerized communications combined with a global push for further financial deregulation in the early 1980s to open the doors to speculative investment. A decade later, the World Bank, the IMF and the US Treasury preached the benefits of liberal financial markets, pressing Third World governments to open their stock markets and financial services – banks, insurance companies, bond dealers and the like.

As noted, the original Bretton Woods agreements specifically sought to limit the movement of finance capital and contain it within national borders. Article VI of the original IMF Articles of Agreement allows members 'to exercise such controls as are necessary to regulate international capital movements'.

Under pressure from what Columbia University economist, Jagdish Bhagwati, calls the 'Wall Street/Treasury' complex, governments in the early 1980s began to dismantle controls on both the flow of investment capital and profits across their borders. Bhagwati argues that lax capital controls serve the 'self-interest' of financiers by enlarging the area in which they can make money.[2]

At the same time the financial services industry itself underwent an unprecedented revolution, sparking a wave of mergers, acquisitions and overseas expansion. In most countries, banks, trust companies, insurance companies and investment brokerages were given the right to fight for each other's business and to compete across international borders. This level of deregulation had not been witnessed in Western countries since the Depression of the 1930s.

The growth in the finance industry was closely linked to the micro-electronics revolution. Computerization means currency traders can move millions of dollars around the world instantly with a few taps on a computer keyboard. Investors profit from minute fluctuations in the price of currencies. The result is what Filipino activist Walden Bello calls a global arbitrage – a game 'where capital moves from one market to another, seeking profits... by taking advantage of interest-rate differentials, targeting gaps between nominal currency values and the "real" currency values, and short-selling in stocks – borrowing shares to artificially inflate share values, then selling.' Volatility is central to this high-tech world of instant millions and Bello, among others, argues that it has become the driving force of the global capitalist system as a whole.[3]

Besides speculating in foreign exchange markets, money managers may also choose to put their funds into direct investment or portfolio investment. Foreign direct investment (FDI) – which tends to be stable and more long term – occurs when foreigners buy equity in local companies, when they purchase existing companies or when they actually start up a new factory or business. Foreign portfolio investment (FPI) – which is typically more volatile – is when foreigners buy shares in the local stock market. The trouble begins because portfolio investors have few ties to bind them to the countries in which their funds are invested. In the current global system where liberalized financial markets are the norm there are no constraints to prohibit investors from selling when they've turned a quick profit or exiting at the first signs of financial difficulties.

Portfolio investment

UNCTAD documented the shift from FDI to FPI during the 1990s. According to their 1998 *World Investment Report*, FPI accounted for a third of all private investment in developing countries from 1990 to 1997. And in some countries like Argentina, Brazil, Mexico, Thailand and South Korea portfolio investment actually outstripped direct investment. The UN agency notes that increasing FPI can signal a more volatile global economy because portfolio investors are 'attracted not so much by the prospect of long-term growth as by the prospect of immediate gain'. Thus they are prone to herd behavior which can lead to 'massive withdrawals' in a crisis.

And crises we've seen – since the 1997 meltdown in Asia there have been financial crises in Russia, Brazil, Turkey and Argentina. All of them required active intervention by international financial institutions and national governments to keep the world system from collapsing.

The Southeast Asian crisis was a wake-up call. It began in mid-1997 when 'hot money' panicked and fled as quickly as it had arrived. Although the IMF and the US Government eventually stepped in with an emergency bailout of more than $120 billion, the damage was widespread. Currencies were devalued in Thailand, Indonesia, the Philippines and South Korea; factories were shut down, imports slashed, workers laid off and public sector services like healthcare, education and transport cut drastically.

As the UN Development Program commented in its 1999 *Human Development Report*: 'The East Asian crisis in not an isolated accident, it is a symptom of general weakness in global capital markets.' The UN agency was not alone in its assessment. Even the pro-business magazine, *The Economist*, admitted that abrupt reversals in capital 'have challenged the conventional wisdom that it is a good thing to let capital move freely across borders'. Others like Professor Bhagwati were less equivocal. 'The Asian crisis cannot be separated from excessive borrowings of foreign short-term capital... It has become apparent that crises attendant on capital mobility cannot be ignored.'

Freefall in Southeast Asia

The Southeast Asian economy went into freefall in the summer of 1997. In the 18 months prior to the crash more short-term investment had entered the region than in the previous ten years. Capital flows into Thailand and Malaysia in the 1990s amounted to more than 10 per cent of Gross Domestic Product (GDP) and most of that 'hot money' went into short-term debt. Previously, these nations had been more cautious about foreign investment and had taken steps to develop domestic industry by closing the door to cheaper imports from the West.

All that changed in the 1990s when these Southeast Asian countries became star pupils of the so-called 'Washington Consensus'. Both the IMF and the World Bank had advised the countries to deregulate their capital accounts as a way of enticing foreign investment and kick-starting the development process. Around 1990 Thailand, Malaysia, Indonesia and the Philippines all adopted an open-door policy to foreign investment. Measures included jacking up domestic interest rates to attract portfolio investment and pegging the national currency to the dollar to ensure that foreign investors wouldn't get hit in case of sudden shifts in the value of the currency.

Hot money

In one of the most thorough examinations of the impact of 'hot money' on national economies, Walden Bello outlines the case of Thailand. In 1994 the World Bank noted in its annual report that 'Thailand provides an excellent example of the dividends to be obtained through outward orientation, receptivity to foreign investment and a market-friendly philosophy backed up by conservative macro-economic management and cautious external borrowing policies.'

Ironically, it was in Thailand that the economic boom first began to fizzle – sparked by the herd mentality of short-term investors. Bello notes that in 1992-1993 the country gave in to IMF pressure and adopted a radical deregulation of its financial system.[4] Measures included: fewer constraints on the portfolio management of financial institutions and commercial banks; looser rules on the expansion of the business of banks and financial institutions; dismantling of foreign exchange controls; and the establishment of

(handwritten margin note, rotated: to handle situation)

the Bangkok International Banking Facility (BIBF). The BIBF was a way for both local and foreign banks to take part in offshore and onshore lending. Firms licensed by the BIBF could both accept deposits and make loans in foreign currencies, to residents and non-residents. Most of the foreign capital entering the country soon came in the form of BIBF dollar loans.

(handwritten margin note, rotated: not designed - gov't economy, inflation, quick profits →)

Pinball capital

The problem was that the capital flooding into Thailand was neither patient nor rooted. Most of it was invested not in goods-producing industries but in areas where profits were reckoned to be sizable and quick. Millions flooded into the stock market (which inflated prices beyond the value of their true worth) and into real estate and various kinds of easy consumer credit like car financing. By late 1996 there was an estimated $24 billion in 'hot money' in Bangkok alone. As a result of this offshore investment the country's foreign debt ballooned from $21 billion in 1988 to $89 billion in 1996. The vast majority of this – more than 80 per cent – was owed to the private sector.[5]

It was a similar story throughout the region. South Korea's foreign debt nearly tripled from $44 billion to $120 billion from 1993 to 1997 – nearly 70 per cent of that was in short-term, easily withdrawn funds. In Indonesia, companies outside the financial sector built up $40 billion in debt by the middle of 1997, 87 per cent of which was short-term. According to official figures the five countries in the region (Indonesia, Thailand, Malaysia, the Philippines and South Korea) had a combined debt to foreign banks of $274 billion just before the crisis: 64 per cent of that was in short-term obligations. This was a recipe for financial disaster.

Much of the speculative capital in Thailand went into real estate, always a favorite for those with a get-rich-quick dream in mind. So much money was pumped into Thai real estate that the value of unsold office buildings and apartments in the country nudged $20 billion. It was this massive bubble that finally frayed the nerves of foreign investors. When they woke up to the fact that most of their money was tied up in property, for which there were no buyers, and that Thai banks were carrying billions in bad debt that could not be serviced, investors panicked and hurried to withdraw their funds. The anxiety (later dubbed the 'contagion effect') spread quickly from Thailand and Malaysia to Indonesia, the Philippines and South Korea. Like the black plague in medieval Europe, this financial chaos was felt to be a contagious disease which could jump national borders.

In just over a year there was a complete turnaround in the capital account of the region: in 1996 new financial inflows to the five countries totaled $93 billion. In 1997, $105 billion left those same countries – a net outflow of $12 billion. All investors rushed for the exit at the same time because none of them wanted to get caught with depreciated local currency and assets.[6]

Downward spiral

The vicious downward spiral picked up speed – egged on by speculators who intervened massively in foreign exchange markets and helped seriously devalue local currencies. Under speculative attack the governments of the region did what they could to ward off the inevitable. The first line of defense was to raid their own foreign exchange reserves to buy up their national currency in the market, in a last-ditch attempt to maintain its value. Under pressure from speculators the Bank of Thailand lost almost all its $38.7 billion in foreign exchange holdings in just six months. But to no avail. Speculators continued to bail out in droves. The next step was to float their currencies but that too backfired, proving a catalyst for further devaluation. The *baht* lost half its value in a few months. So the hemorrhage of foreign funds helped both to deplete foreign exchange reserves and to drive down the value of domestic currencies.

The Thai baht felt the pressure first but the devaluation soon spread to the other countries. As the currency drifted downwards, local firms who had borrowed from abroad had to pay more in local currency for the foreign exchange needed to service their overseas debts. At the first sign that things were spinning out of control many foreign banks and other creditors refused to roll over their loans. They demanded immediate repayment. At this point the panic that gripped the region suddenly became a crisis threatening to capsize the entire global economy. Soon, international financial operators were selling *baht*, *ringgit* and *rupiah* in an effort to cut potential losses and get their funds safely back to Europe and the US. In the ensuing capital flight, Asian stock prices plunged and the value of local currencies collapsed. Businesses that had taken out dollar-denominated loans couldn't afford the dollar payments to Western creditors.

For a time governments tried to stave off default by lending some of their foreign currency reserves to the indebted private companies. South Korea used up some $30 billion in this way. But the money soon ran out and Western banks refused to make new loans or roll over old debts. Asian businesses defaulted, cutting output and laying off workers. As the region's economies sputtered, panic intensified. Asian currencies lost 35 to 85 per cent of their foreign-exchange value, driving up prices on imported goods and pushing down the standard of living. Businesses large and small were driven to bankruptcy by the sudden drying up of credit; within a year, millions of workers had lost jobs while prices of imports, including basic foodstuffs, soared.

Calming investors
In an effort to calm investors and forestall total financial collapse the International Monetary Fund (IMF)

was called in with a $120 billion bailout plan. But the IMF rescue package actually succeeded in making a bad situation worse – not least for the citizens of those nations who had to endure the impact of the Fund's edict. One of the central requirements of the package was that governments guarantee continued debt service payments to the private sector in return for the agency persuading creditors to roll over or restructure their loans. This mirrored the IMF's role during the Third World debt crisis of the 1980s. Public money from Northern taxpayers (via the Fund) was handed over to indebted governments, then recycled to commercial banks in the South to pay off their debts to private investors. In Asia this bailout of international creditors was dubbed 'socialism for the global financial élite' by some critics.

The Fund's Asian package also forced countries to further liberalize their capital account. The goal was to cut government expenditure and produce a surplus. The standard tools were applied: high interest rates combined with cuts to both government expenditures and subsidies to basics like food, fuel and transport. The high interest rates were supposed to be the bait to lure back foreign capital so all would be well again. But the bait didn't work. Tight domestic credit combined with high interest rates sparked a much sharper recession than would have otherwise taken place and did nothing to restore investor confidence.

Output in some countries fell 16 per cent or more, unemployment soared and wages nose-dived. In Thailand GDP growth-rate estimates plummeted after the IMF intervention, from 2.5 per cent in August 1997 to minus 3.5 per cent in February 1998. In Indonesia the IMF forced the Government to close down 16 banks, a move it thought would restore confidence in the notoriously inefficient banking system. Instead it led to panic withdrawals by customers at remaining banks which brought further chaos. It is estimated that half the businesses in the country went bankrupt.

The set-back for development was so severe that non-governmental agencies estimated it would take a decade or longer to make-up the lost ground. Oxfam analyzed the situation as follows: 'The crisis now gripping East Asia bears comparison in terms of its destructive impact with the Great Depression of 1929. What started as a financial crisis has been allowed to develop into a full-fledged social and economic crisis, with devastating consequences for human development. Previously rising incomes have been reversed and unemployment and underemployment have reached alarming levels. Rising food prices and falling social spending have further aggravated the social conditions of the poorest.'[7]

The impact of the crisis was stunning. According to the International Labor Organization (ILO) more than 20 million people in Indonesia were laid off from September 1997 to September 1998. UNICEF said that 250,000 clinics there were closed and predicted that infant mortality would jump by 30 per cent. The Asian Development Bank said that more than 6 million children dropped out of school. And Oxfam estimated that over 100 million Indonesians were living in poverty a year after the crisis – four times more than two years earlier.

There was also a frightening resurgence of racial 'scape-goating' and inter-communal violence throughout the region. Malaysia's leader at this time, the autocratic Mahathir Mohamad, blamed Jewish financiers for destabilizing his Muslim country, while in Indonesia the shops of ethnic-Chinese merchants were looted and burned and hundreds of Chinese brutally beaten and killed.

There were, however, some clear winners that emerged from the Asian meltdown. The big ones were the Western corporate interests that rushed in to snap up the region's bargain-basement assets after the economic collapse. As former US Trade Representative Mickey Kantor said at the time, the recession in the 'Tiger Economies' was a golden chance for the West to reassert its commercial interests. 'When countries seek help from the IMF,' he said, 'Europe and America should use the IMF as a battering ram to gain advantage.'[8]

South Korea

That was certainly true in South Korea where the IMF agreement lifted restrictions on outside ownership so that foreigners could purchase up to 55 per cent of Korean companies and 100 per cent of Korean banks. Years of effort by the Korean élite to keep businesses firmly under control of state-supported conglomerates called chaebols were undone in a matter of months. In January 1998 the French investment firm Credit Lyonnais estimated that just 87 of the country's 653 non-financial firms were safe from foreign buyers. Rudi Dornbusch, a US economist, accurately summed up the overall impact of the economic crisis. 'Korea is now owned and operated by our Treasury. That's the positive side of this crisis.'[9]

A key reason why the Asian economies were so vulnerable to currency destabilization was that they had gradually abandoned controls over the movement of capital. When a country cedes its control over capital flows it effectively removes any tools it may have for intervening in the market process, leaving itself at the mercy of speculators whose only concern is profit. More critically, nations lose the ability to control internal economic strategies which lie at the heart of national sovereignty. How can a nation hope to determine its own social agenda and economic future if key policy areas are shaped by the self-interest of foreign investors and money markets?

At the time of the Asian meltdown, one country emerged from the chaos in noticeably better shape than the others. Although Malaysia's GDP fell by 7.5

per cent in 1998, the nation managed to escape the devastating social impact felt elsewhere. Partly this was because Malaysia adopted a range of defensive measures to limit capital flight, many of which were modeled on the Chinese example.

The Malaysian Central Bank ruled that private companies could only contract foreign loans if they could show that the loans would end up producing foreign exchange which then could be used to service the debt. And like China, Malaysia also pegged its currency, the *ringgit*, to the US dollar and allowed it to be freely con-

---

Market buzz

A pocket guide to the language of the financial market place.

• **Hedging**

If a business holds stocks of a commodity like cocoa or copper it runs the risk of losing money if the price falls before it can unload it all. This loss can be avoided by 'hedging' the risk. This involves selling the item before the purchaser actually wants it – ie for delivery at an agreed price at a future date. Hedge funds make a business of selling and buying this risk, often using borrowed money to put together 'highly leveraged' deals. The most infamous hedge fund, the US firm Long Term Capital Management (LTCM), had to be rescued with a $3.5 billion bailout from other Wall Street investment companies after it overextended itself to the tune of $200 billion. The firm had invested $500 million of borrowed money for every million dollars it invested of its own cash.

• **Futures, options and swaps**

A futures contract is an agreement to buy or sell a commodity or shares or currency at a future date at a price decided when the contract is first agreed. An option is like a futures contract except that in this case there is a right, but no obligation, to trade at an agreed price at a future date. An interest-rate swap is a transaction by which financial institutions change the form of their assets or debts. Swaps can be between fixed and floating rate debt, or between debt in different currencies.

• **Derivatives**

A sweeping, catchall term used to refer to a range of extremely complex and obscure financial arrangements. Futures contracts, futures on stock market indices, options and swaps are all derivatives. In general, derivatives are tradable securities whose value is 'derived' (thus the name) from some underlying instrument which may be a stock, bond, commodity or currency. They can be used as a hedge to reduce risks or for speculation. According to the Bank for International Settlements the notional value of

---

verted to other foreign currencies for trade and direct investment. However, portfolio investors had to keep their funds inside Malaysia for a minimum of one year and the amount of money residents could take out of the country was restricted.

Most importantly, trade in *ringgit* outside the country was not recognized by the Government and this helped to prevent manipulation by currency speculators. Measures were also taken to reduce foreign investment in the Malaysian stock market. The controls allowed the Government to stimulate the domestic economy

---

all derivatives in effect in June 2004 was $221 trillion which dwarfs the value of all the world's stock markets combined.

• **Stock market indices**

The most famous are the Dow Jones Industrial Average, an index of share prices on the US stock market based on 30 leading US companies, the FTSE 100, an index of Britain's 100 top companies and the Japanese equivalent, the NIKKEI 225.

• **Foreign exchange market**

This is where currencies are traded. There is no single location for this market since it operates via computer and telephone connections in an interlaced web linking hundreds of trading points all over the world. The total turnover of world foreign exchange markets is enormous, many times the total international trade in goods and services.

• **Mutual funds/Unit trusts**

A financial institution which holds shares on behalf of investors. The investors buy shares or 'units' in the fund, which uses their money to buy shares in a range of companies. An investor selling back the units gets the proceeds of selling a fraction of the fund's total portfolio rather than just shares in one or two companies.

• **Equities**

The ordinary shares or common stock of companies. The owners of these shares are entitled to the residual profits of companies after all claims of creditors, debenture holders and preference shareholders have been satisfied. These are paid out to stock owners in the form of dividends.

• **Junk bonds**

Bonds issued on very doubtful security by firms where there is serious doubt as to whether interest and redemption payments will actually be made. Because these bonds are so risky, lenders are only prepared to hold them if promised returns are high enough. ■

with tax cuts, lower interest rates and spending on public infrastructure – without having to worry about speculators targeting its currency. Interest rates fell from 11 to 7 per cent, a helpful boon to local businesses and the domestic banking industry.

China's response

Despite its authoritarian political structure China was also able to sidestep the Asian trap – mainly by avoiding becoming entangled in international financial markets. At the time of the Asian financial crisis China had considerably more control over its domestic economy than just about any nation in the world. Its currency, the *renmimbi*, was not freely convertible; its finance system was domestically owned and controlled by the State and there was relatively little foreign investment in the Chinese stock market. Plus the world's biggest nation was not then a member of the WTO – the country finally became a full member of the organization in December 2001.

As a result China was not vulnerable to the speculative herd behavior that devastated other countries in the region. Instead of devaluing its currency and trying to grab a share of its neighbors' exports, China took another tack. The Government decided to direct national savings into a $200 billion public works program to stimulate its domestic economy.[10]

Chile is another country that successfully tried to regulate destabilizing short-term flows of foreign capital by installing a series of financial 'speed bumps' to slow down speculation. When Mexico's economy crashed in 1995 Chile was able to escape the worst 'contagion' effects because of its *encaje* policy. This regulation required foreign investors to deposit funds equivalent to 30 per cent of their investment in Chile's central bank. In addition, portfolio investors were required to keep their cash inside the country for a minimum of at least a year. These barriers slowed down the exodus of funds from Chile and kept it from falling victim to what the financial press dubbed Mexico's 'tequila effect'.

Shaken by the Asian débâcle Western finance ministers, led by the US, came up with a new plan to aid countries experiencing balance-of-payments shortfalls before such a crisis occurs. The idea was to give more money (up to $90 billion) and more power to the IMF to create 'an enhanced IMF facility for countries pursuing strong IMF-approved policies'. The thinking was that an instant loan from a 'precautionary fund' would make currency speculators less anxious and so tame the 'hot money' and stall devaluation.

Brazilian crash

Brazil was the first country to use the new IMF plan. Unfortunately, Brazil's economy seemed no more immune to financial crisis than Indonesia or Thailand. When the Brazilian *real* came under attack in 1998 the government of Fernando Cardoso spent more than $40 billion in foreign exchange trying to prop it up. Cardoso also raised domestic interest rates to 50 per cent to try to keep capital from fleeing the country. Nevertheless traders continued to hammer the *real* even after the country signed a formal letter of intent with the IMF. By January 1999 nearly a billion dollars a day was exiting the country – the Government had no choice but to finally devalue its currency which lost nearly a third of its value overnight.

The Brazilian economy went crashing as IMF policies kicked in. High interest rates scared off domestic business owners who could no longer afford to borrow. Budget cuts and public sector layoffs increased poverty and unemployment as the Government was forced to implement what the IMF called 'the largest privatization program in history'. As in Asia the IMF/US Treasury plan championed foreign investment, lured by high interest rates, as Brazil's only long-term hope. Unfortunately, the Fund brushed aside the downside of interest rate hikes – each percentage increase adds millions to debt service costs, all of which have to be repaid in hard currencies purchased with the devalued Brazilian real. By the end of 1999 Brazil's total external debt, always the highest in the South, topped more than $230 billion.

Argentina takes a stand

The next South American nation to feel the pinch of financial liberalization was Argentina, one of the first Latin nations to fervently embrace globalization. In December 2001 the country sent shock waves around the world when the economy exploded into social chaos. In less than two weeks five different presidents tried to take control and calm the increasingly violent demonstrations which had erupted across the country. '*Que se vayan todos!*' the protestors chanted: 'Out with the lot of them!' – meaning all the politicians and the international financiers that had helped bring the country to its knees.

The crisis had its roots in the economic model pushed by the IMF in the early 1990s when Carlos Menem was President. In return for emergency balance-of-payments support Argentina knocked down its trade barriers, liberalized its capital account and instituted a massive privatization of state enterprises. Nearly 400 companies from oil and water to steel, insurance, telephone and postal services were sold off to foreign interests. Corruption was rife: Menem and his cronies grew rich in the process.

But what really attracted speculators was the government's move to peg the Argentine *peso* to the US dollar at an exchange rate of one-to-one. This effectively removed all control over the domestic economy from the hands of the government. The IMF happily endorsed the arrangement.

Then things began to unravel. With a fixed exchange rate and the dollar rising in value Argentine goods quickly became uncompetitive, both globally and locally. Cheaper imports flooded the country as the once-thriving agricultural sector slumped. Even the world-famous Argentine beef industry saw export markets dry up. The country had to borrow more foreign currency to finance the growing trade gap, further increasing an already heavy debt burden. Soon lenders began to get the jitters, credit disappeared and businesses lurched into bankruptcy.

In December 2001 Argentina again approached the IMF for a loan to meet its $140 billion external debt. When the Fund balked, the country defaulted on $100 billion of its debt, and then quickly spiraled into recession. In a few short months unemployment spiked to 21 per cent, GDP declined nearly 17 per cent and more than half of Argentines were living below the poverty line. Something had to give.

Fed up with political corruption and destructive impact of foreign debt, the Argentine people began to demand more control over their economic lives. The collapse sparked a flurry of worker-run enterprises, co-operatives, alternative currencies, barter exchanges and other self-help institutions. More than 200 companies were taken over and managed by their employees after owners shut up shop.

In May 2003 the populist government of Nestor Kirchner was elected. In a bold move Kirchner told debtors he would write off 75 per cent of his country's $100 billion in defaulted government bonds – take it or leave it. In September 2003 he also convinced the IMF to roll over $21 billion in outstanding debt, insisting that no more than 3 per cent of the nation's budget would be used for debt servicing. Pushed to the wall the IMF caved in.

'We are not going to repeat the history of the past,' said Kirchner. 'For many years we were on our knees before financial organizations and the speculative funds... We've had enough!'[11]

Global casino

In a stunning turnaround the country finally cleared its account with the Fund in January 2006 repaying $9.57 billion in debt and gaining a measure of economic autonomy not felt for decades.

It wasn't easy. Argentina got no help from the IMF along the way. The Fund opposed policies that led to recovery – a stable exchange rate, low interest rates and a tax on exports. A stable currency was important to keep the *peso* from becoming overvalued. Priced competitively, exports would grow and encourage local investment. Instead the IMF wanted to increase the price of public services like water and electricity, run bigger budget surpluses and pay off foreign creditors. But the Kirchner government held fast – and the economy responded by growing by nearly 9 per cent yearly from 2003 to 2006. This was an amazing accomplishment, all the more so because the country continued to service its other debts during that time.

The search for solutions

Despite the obvious danger of capital ricocheting around the globe, the IMF and the US Treasury have been reluctant to support mechanisms to inhibit its movement. And speculators themselves have also been working overtime to squelch defensive government action against their attacks. Pressures to lift exchange controls have increased despite repeated crises and heavy criticism.

The original Bretton Woods agreement did not fulfill Keynes' dream of giving 'every member government the explicit right to control capital movements' but the policies did give members some controls. Unfortunately, even these limited tools have been gradually eroded over the years by the growing insistence on deregulation. Market fundamentalists like former US Treasury official Lawrence Summers (now President of Harvard University) criticized efforts by Malaysia, Hong Kong and others to hobble the movement of overseas capital.

He called controls a 'catastrophe' and urged countries to 'open up to foreign financial service providers, and all the competition, capital and expertise they bring with them'. Given the damage inflicted on millions by the fickle nature of short-term speculators, Summers' views are both short-sighted and harmful.

As citizens from Korea to Argentina see their lives wrecked by the whipsaw effect of one global financial crisis after another it is becoming painfully evident that the old ways no longer work. The world has been led to the brink of financial chaos too often over the last few decades. Solutions are needed urgently to ensure that money markets, bond traders and currency speculators are brought under the control of national governments for the public good.

1 See 'Questions and Answers' at www.stampoutpoverty.org. **2** 'The Capital Myth: the difference between the trade in widgets and the trade in dollars', Jagdish Bhagwati, *Foreign Affairs*, May/June 1998. **3** *Dilemmas of Domination*, Walden Bello (Zed Books, London, 2005). **4** 'Domesticating Markets: A social justice perspective on the debate over a new global financial architecture', by Walden Bello, *Multinational Monitor*, March 1999. **5** Testimony of Walden Bello before the House Banking Committee, US House of Representatives, 21 April 1998. **6** *Human Development Report 1999* (UN Development Program/Oxford University Press). **7** Oxfam East Asia Briefing, available from www.oxfam.org.uk. **8** Quoted in 'Globalization for Whom?', Mark Weisbrot, Research Director, Preamble Center, www.preamble.org/globalization. **9** Quoted in 'Asian Crisis Spurs Search for New Global Rules', *Economic Justice Report*, July 1998. **10** 'The Case for National Economic Sovereignty', Mark Weisbrot, Third World Network Features, July 1999. **11** 'Can't pay, won't pay', Roger Burbach, *New Internationalist* No374 December 2004.

6 Poverty, the environment and the market

Faith in economic growth as the key to progress comes into question as the earth's life-support systems fray and signs of ecological collapse multiply. Globalization, geared to spur rapid growth through greater resource consumption, is straining the environment and widening gaps between rich and poor. The standard cure of orthodox market economics – privatization, tax cuts and foreign investment – is not effective. Criticism and concern grows from both expert-insiders and grassroots communities.

WHETHER THEY ARE disciples of Keynes, confirmed free-marketers or top-down central planners, economists of all stripes have an abiding faith in the healing powers of economic growth. Keynesians opt for government regulation and an active fiscal policy to kick-start growth in times of economic malaise. They believe the impact of state spending will catalyze the economy, create jobs and stimulate consumption. Keynesians (and the Left in general) have been concerned with making sure that the growing economic pie was distributed fairly. Socialists and some trade unionists have held out for more control over the production process by workers themselves.

Market fundamentalists, sometimes called 'neoliberals', hope to boost consumption using different levers. They opt for 'pure' market solutions – tax cuts and low interest rates – both of which are supposed to increase spending and investment by putting more money into peoples' pockets.

But, until recently, all sides have ignored the environment. The increasingly global economy is completely dependent on the larger economy of the planet Earth. And evidence is all around us that the planet's ecological health is in trouble.

Our system of industrial production has chewed through massive quantities of non-renewable natural resources over the past two centuries. Not only are we wiping out ecosystems and habitats at an alarming rate, but it is also clear that we are exploiting our natural resource base (the economy's 'natural capital') and generating waste at a rate which exceeds the capacity of the natural world to regenerate and heal itself.

We don't have to look far for proof that growth-centered economics is pushing the regenerative capacities of the planet's ecosystems to the brink. While there is concern that the supply of oil – the most essential, non-renewable resource for the industrialized economy – has already peaked, there is no shortage of other raw materials. Even at current rates of consumption there is enough copper, iron and nickel to last centuries. More pressing is the disintegration of the basic life-support systems that we take for granted. The water cycle, the composition of the atmosphere, the assimilation of waste and recycling of nutrients, the pollination of crops, and the delicate interplay of species: all these are in danger.

There is now a large body of research documenting this precipitous decline. Deserts are spreading, forests being hacked down, fertile soils ruined by erosion and desalinization, fisheries exhausted, species pushed to extinction, ground water reserves pumped dry. Carbon dioxide levels in the atmosphere continue to rise due to our extravagant burning of fossil fuels. The Intergovernmental Panel on Climate Change, a select group of nearly 2,500 of the world's top climate scientists, says that climate change is unstoppable and will lead to 'widespread economic, social and environmental dislocation over the next century'. The UN's Millennium Ecosystem Assessment, released in March 2005, was a stark warning that human activity is putting such strain on the natural functions of the Earth that the ability of the planet's ecosystems to sustain future generations can no longer be taken for granted.

The World Conservation Union's (IUCN) Year 2000 Red List of Threatened Species warned that the global extinction crisis is accelerating, with dramatic declines in populations of many species, including reptiles and primates. The Swiss-based IUCN sees habitat loss, human exploitation and invasion by alien species as major threats to wildlife. This loss of habitat is affecting 89 per cent of all threatened birds, 83 per cent of threatened mammals and 91 per cent of threatened plants. The highest number of threatened mammals and birds are found in lowland and mountain tropical rain forests where 900 bird species and 55 per cent of all mammals are threatened.

The UN concludes we are losing species faster than any time in history, at a rate of 1,000 times the natural rate of extinction. Between a third and a half of terrestrial species are expected to die out over the next two centuries if current trends continue unchecked. Scientists reckon the normal extinction rate is one species every four years.[1]

Stealing from the future
Since 1950 global economic output has jumped from $3.8 trillion to nearly $20 trillion, a five-fold increase. We have consumed more of the world's natural capital in this brief period than during the entire history of humankind.

The ecologists William Rees and Mathis Wackernagel pioneered the 'ecological footprint' concept which attempts to put a number on the amount of ecological space occupied by people and by nations. They estimate that around 4-6 hectares of land are used to maintain the consumption of the average person in the West. However, the total available productive land in the world is about 1.7 hectares per person (total land divided by population). The difference Rees calls 'appropriated carrying capacity' – which basically

Humanity's footprint

The world's demand is outstripping the earth's biocapacity so we are now beginning to consume irreplaceable natural capital. According to ecologist William Rees the global footprint exceeds the earth's biological capacity by 20% and the gap is growing steadily every year.

Demand vs. Biocapacity

Footprint (number of planets)

1.5

1.0

0.5

0

1961   1971   1981   1991   2001

—— World Biocapacity   —— Demand

http://www.footprintnetwork.org

means the rich are living off the resources of the poor.

The Netherlands, for example, consumes the output of a productive land mass 14 times its size. Most Northern countries and many urban regions in the South already consume more than their fair share; they depend on trade (using someone else's natural assets) or on depleting their own natural capital. According to Rees and Wackernagel the global footprint now exceeds global biocapacity by 20 per cent and that gap is growing yearly. The US alone, with 4.5 per cent of the world's population, sucks up 25 per cent of the earth's biocapacity. The average Indian has a global footprint of just 0.8 hectares while the average American has an ecological footprint of 9.7 hectares.[2]

Regions like North America and Western Europe, argue Rees and Wackernagel, 'run an unaccounted ecological deficit – their population either appropriating carrying capacity from elsewhere or from future generations'.[3]

Faith in economic growth as the ultimate hope

for human progress is widespread. A central tenet of economists on the Left and Right has been that the 'carrying capacity' of the Earth is infinitely expandable. The underlying belief is that a combination of ingenuity and technology will eventually allow us all to live like middle-class Americans – if only we can only ignore the naysayers and keep the economy growing.

Unfortunately, this doesn't look likely. As the Worldwatch Institute points out: 'Rising demand for energy, food and raw materials by 2.5 billion Chinese and Indians is already having ripple effects worldwide... If China and India were to consume resources and produce pollution at the current US per capita level, it would require two planet Earths just to sustain their two economies.'[2]

Says ecologist Robert Ayres: 'There is every indication that human economic activity supported by perverse trade and growth policies is well on the way to perturbing our natural environment more and faster than any known event in planetary history.'[4]

Ayres is on to something when he accuses the 'perverse' aspects of globalization as accelerating the process of environmental decline. Export-led growth and Third World debt have combined to speed up the rapid consumption of the Earth's irreplaceable natural resources. Some environmentalists argue that primary resources (nature's goods and services) are too cheap and that their market price does not reflect either their finite nature or the hidden social and ecological costs of extraction. Instead, they suggest, we should conserve the resources we have by making them more expensive. There is some truth to this analysis. The price of raw materials is notoriously unpredictable, based not just on supply and demand but also on the monopoly power of corporations that control distribution and sales. In recent years the price of industrial metals like nickel, copper and iron has risen in tandem with the Chinese economy. On the other hand world-market prices for other commodities like cotton, sugar and coffee have never been lower.

Prices plummeted during the Asian financial crisis. But debt in the developing countries, the source of many of the world's commodities, has also kept prices low. Centuries of colonialism put in place a system of extreme dependency on a narrow range of primary exports which remains to this day. According to UNCTAD, just three commodities account for 75 per cent of total exports in each of the 48 poorest nations. This might be tolerable if nations like Honduras, Kenya and Zambia earned a decent income from their sugar, tea and copper. Sadly, the opposite is true. Due to plunging 'terms of trade' commodity-dependent nations need to export more and more every year just to stay in the same place. From 1997 to 2001 the combined price index of all commodities fell by 53 per cent – raw exports lost half their purchasing power in terms of manufactured goods.

'Adjustment' policies imposed by the IMF/World Bank as the price of admission to the global trading community mean that poor countries are obliged to service their debts before they are allowed to do anything else. They have little choice but to try and expand commodity exports to world markets. Unfortunately, removing the barriers to Third World exports isn't always the answer. In fact, it can make matters worse, especially in the agricultural sector. When farmers grow more for export, it often leads, perversely, to over-production and lower prices. Faced with lower earnings farmers respond rationally by increasing their production to earn more. Added to this desperate cycle is the black hole of debt: countries in hock have been forced by World Bank and IMF structural adjustment edicts to ratchet up exports to service their debts. The new term circulating among critical economists to describe the phenomenon is 'immiserating trade'. The more you trade, the poorer you get.[5]

Poverty, the environment and the market

And therein lies the problem. Because all poor countries have to increase their exports at once, there is a glut and prices fall – sometimes by half. Twice as much has to be exported to earn the same amount of foreign currency. The beneficiaries are the developed countries and Western-based corporations. They not only get their debts serviced, but they also benefit from cheap commodities that keep prices down, profits up and inflation under control in the North. The losers are the people of the South – who depend on primary exports – and the global environment.

Deregulated destruction

Globalization policies put the squeeze on the environment in other ways, too. Take the case of Brazil which environmentalists consider one of the earth's most ecologically important nations. The country still contains 30 per cent of the planet's rainforest long considered to be 'the lungs of the world'. Scientists believe the spectacular biological diversity of the rainforest is a potential cornucopia of priceless, life-saving drugs.

In 1999 the Brazilian Government slashed millions of dollars off environmental spending in the wake of IMF-enforced cuts. The country's environmental enforcement arm had its budget reduced by 19 per cent. In addition the domestic recession brought on by IMF policies boosted unemployment, forcing many ordinary workers and peasants to clear larger areas of jungle for subsistence.

Encouraging primary exports can also strengthen the hand of agribusiness and large landowners. Peasant farmers and smallholders are squeezed out by the implacable logic of economic efficiency. In Brazil the amount of land devoted to large-scale soy production has jumped from 200,000 hectares to 12 million hectares over the past 30 years, much of it virgin rainforest. The growth of the country's beef industry has caused even more environmental destruction in the Amazon. In 2004, 26,000 sq km of rainforest was burned, the second highest rate on record, mostly due to cattle ranching. Brazil is now the world's biggest beef exporter but the industry's continued expansion threatens 40 per cent of the world's remaining rainforest.[6]

Gustavo Fonseca of the Center for Biological Science at the Washington-based Conservation International sums up the concern of environmentalists: 'Our biggest worry now is that the Government is going to lose control of attempts to control deforestation. This is undermining the very basis of what we've been trying to accomplish in Brazil.'[7]

Even before the crash of 1997, part of Asia's 'economic miracle' had been built on a fast-track liquidation of its natural resources. Pristine rainforests were plundered, rivers despoiled, seacoasts poisoned with pesticides and fisheries exhausted. In the Indonesian capital, Jakarta, more than 70 per cent of water samples were found to be 'highly contaminated by chemical pollutants' while the country's forests were being hacked down at the rate of 6 million acres (2.4 million hectares) per year. In the Malaysian state of Sarawak (part of the island of Borneo) 30 per cent of the forest disappeared in a mere two decades, while in peninsular Malaysia 73 per cent of 116 rivers surveyed by authorities were found to be either 'biologically dead' or 'dying'.[8]

The environmental group, Friends of the Earth (FoE), summarized the impact of free-market deregulation on Third World environments in its 1999 study, *IMF: Selling the Environment Short*. FoE examined IMF policies in eight countries including Cameroon, Côte d'Ivoire, Guyana, Nicaragua and Thailand and found significant negative environmental impacts in all of them.

Spending cuts
Several countries slashed government spending after

being pressured by the Fund to eliminate budget deficits. The report also noted that IMF policies encourage, and sometimes induce, countries to exploit natural resources at unsustainable rates. According to Carol Welch, co-author of the report and International Policy Analyst at Friends of the Earth: 'Every case shows that the IMF pushes short-term profit at the expense of biodiversity and ecological prosperity... the IMF is undermining people's lives by disregarding environmental issues.'[9]

Persistent poverty has also spurred environmental decline – the desperately poor do not make good eco-citizens. Tribal peoples plunder the forest on which they depend for survival; animals are poached and slaughtered by impoverished African villagers for their valuable ivory or their body parts.

Madagascar, an island once covered in lush forests, has turned into a barren wasteland as local people slash-and-burn jungle plots to grow food. The huge Indian Ocean island is home to some 200,000 plant and animal species – three-quarters of which are found nowhere else. Less than a tenth of Madagascar is still tree-covered and the forest is vanishing at the rate of 200,000 hectares a year. Poverty is the core of the problem: 70 per cent of the island's 14 million people live on less than a dollar a day.

'Our village has been burning forests to plant rice here for generations,' Dimanche Dimasy, chief elder of Mahatsara village, told the BBC. 'This is our way of life. If we can't cut the forests, we can't feed ourselves. The government wants to protect the forests but nobody cares about protecting the peasants who live here.'[10]

Cracks in the consensus
The logic of globalization is seductive because it is based on a simple principle: free the market of constraints and its self-evolving dynamic will bring

employment, wealth and prosperity. But despite the confidence of those who preach the gospel of free markets, there are clear indications that some people are losing their faith.

The signs are inescapable – not least of which are the thousands of civil society groups around the world who have begun to take their protests to the streets. More than 50,000 people from dozens of countries demonstrated in Seattle in November 1999 at the annual meeting of the World Trade Organization. The gathering was a unique mix of environmentalists, trade unionists, peasant groups, students and ordinary citizens – all united by their concern that economic globalization is spinning out of control. The protest gained world-wide prominence when police in riot gear charged the crowds, firing pepper gas, tear gas and plastic bullets. Five hundred people were arrested and a state of emergency declared.

Then at the spring meetings of the IMF and World Bank in April 2000 another 15,000 people gathered in Washington for a repeat protest. Ironically the same week, as if to underline the demonstrators' critique of globalization, stock markets nose-dived as a wave of panic-selling swept the globe, puncturing the high-tech stock bubble that had carried markets to dizzying new heights through the 1990s. After Seattle, civil society demonstrations became a regular occurrence at meetings of the Bretton Woods trio or the G8 – Prague in October 2000, Quebec City in April 2001, Genoa in July 2001, Miami in November 2003, Hong Kong in December 2005. Everywhere the proponents of economic globalization now meet they run into a similar phalanx of protesters.

Even among mainstream economists globalization is coming under increasing scrutiny. The financial crises in Russia, Asia and Latin America in the last half of the 1990s opened deep rifts in the dominant 'Washington consensus' – a view which had been advocated by the Bretton Woods institutions and endorsed by most Western governments. Powerful voices that had previously backed free trade and market liberalization began to speak out.

The influential economist Jeffrey Sachs was one of those. Formerly Director of Harvard's Center for International Development, Sachs was an advisor to the IMF, one of the main engineers of capitalist 'shock therapy' in Russia after the fall of the Soviet Union – and a leading voice in favor of economic globalization. The Asian débâcle forced him to re-examine his faith in the supremacy of free markets and to question some of the conventional solutions to national financial crises – especially the role of the IMF. In a candid Financial Times article published in December 1997 Sachs called the IMF 'secretive' and 'unaccountable'. 'It defies logic,' he said, that 'a small group of 1,000 economists on 19th Street in Washington should dictate the economic conditions of life to 75 developing countries with around 1.4 billion people'.

Others began to speak out too. The World Bank's former Chief Economist, Joseph Stiglitz, became a much-quoted 'ex-insider' willing to publicly criticize the conservative policies of market fundamentalists.

Globalization and its Discontents, his scathing 2002 critique of the Bretton Woods institutions, became a bestseller, studded with personal anecdotes and case studies.

'The net effect of the policies set by the Washington consensus,' he wrote, 'has all too often been to benefit the few at the expense of the many, the well-off at the expense of the poor. In many cases commercial interests and values have superseded concern for the environment, democracy, human rights, and social justice.'[11]

As if to reinforce this assessment of spreading 'economic insecurity' the IMF's *World Economic Outlook* report for 2000 noted that despite the spectacular economic growth of the past half century, the quality of life for a fifth of the world's population has actually regressed in relative, and sometimes absolute, terms. One of the most cogent critiques of the downside of globalization comes from the UN Development Program. Its yearly *Human Development Report* is a first-rate compilation of insightful data and cogent, probing analysis. It's not journalism but it gets to the point. 'When the market goes too far in dominating social and political outcomes, the opportunities and rewards of globalization spread unequally and inequitably – concentrating power and wealth in a select group of people, nations and corporations, marginalizing the others.'[12]

Mind the gap

Despite an apparent increase in global growth and steadily increasing per capita income, the gap both within and between rich and poor countries is widening.

- The richest fifth of the world's population receives more than 75% of world income while the poorest 20% receives just 1.5%.
- The richest 50 individuals in the world have a combined income greater than that of the poorest 416 million.
- 2.5 billion people living on less than $2 a day – 40% of the world's population – receive only 5% of global income.
- Of the 73 countries for which figures are available, 53 (with over 80% of the world's population) have seen income inequality increase. In only 9 countries (about 4% of the world's population) has the wealth gap between rich and poor been reduced.

Human Development Report 2005, UN Development Program, New York 2005.

Poverty, the environment and the market

The UN agency supports its analysis with hard-hitting figures on what it calls a 'grotesque and dangerous polarization' between those people and countries benefiting from the system and those that are merely 'passive recipients' of its effects.

Even on its own terms economic globalization is not working for the majority of the world's citizens. As Joseph Stiglitz points outs: 'Despite repeated promises of poverty reduction made over the last decade of the 20th century, the actual number of people living in poverty has actually increased by 100 million.'[11] In 1960, the fifth of the world's people who live in the richest countries had 30 times more income than the fifth living in the poorest countries. By 1997 the income gap had more than doubled. According to UNDP, the top five per cent of the world's population had an income 114 times greater than the bottom five per cent; while the world's richest 500 individuals have a combined income greater than that of the poorest 416 million.

Income inequality is increasing in countries that account for more than 80 per cent of the world's population. And the growing gap can mean life or death: children born into the poorest 20 per cent of households in Ghana or Senegal are two to three times more likely to die before age 5 than children born into the richest 20 per cent of households.[13]

The widening gap

Another UN study, this one on income inequality in OECD countries, concluded that in the 1980s real wages (adjusted for inflation) had fallen and income inequality increased in all countries except Germany and Italy.

In the US, the top ten per cent of families boosted their average income by 16 per cent while the top one per cent increased theirs by a whopping 50 per cent. This trend was echoed elsewhere. In Latin America the top 10 per cent of wage-earners increased their share while the poorest 10 per cent saw their income drop by 15 per cent, wiping out what meager improvements they had made in the previous decade. Income inequality also grew in Thailand, Indonesia, China and other Asian nations even though the region enjoyed healthy economic growth throughout the decade. In Sub-Saharan Africa the situation is worse: after two decades of IMF/World Bank structural adjustment income inequality is not only growing but per capita incomes are falling. UNDP says it will take Sub-Saharan Africa until 2112 just to restore average incomes to their 1980 levels. They are now lower than they were in 1990. The region had 100 million more people living on less than a dollar a day in 2001 than a decade earlier.

This shift in wealth and income from bottom to top is part of the logic of globalization. In order to be 'competitive' governments adopt policies which cut taxes and favor profits over wages. The economic argument is simple: putting more money into the pockets of corporations and wealthy individuals (who benefit most from tax cuts: the higher the income the greater the gain) is supposed to lead to greater investment, jobs, economic growth and prosperity. Corporate tax rates have dropped across the industrialized world over the past decade. According to the Citizens for Tax Justice, effective corporate tax rates in the US dropped from 27 per cent to 17 per cent in the 1988-2003 period.[14]

Unfortunately, there is no evidence that improvements in public well-being result from tax cuts for the rich or lower wages for the rest of us. If the reverse was true and tax cuts were directed towards those at the bottom of the income ladder there might be some impact. The money would almost certainly be spent on basic necessities rather than luxury goods. But this isn't part of the globalization game plan. In every country that has taken up the 'reduce-taxes-cut-the-deficit' mantra the majority of tax cuts benefit wealthy individuals and corporations. What happens to the money is perhaps predictable: some goes into high-priced consumer baubles – a phenomenon which is glaringly visible amongst the élite in cities from Bangkok to Los Angeles. But most winds up in the stock market or in other sorts of non-productive speculative activity.

Major players are no longer satisfied with modest profits on long-term investment, especially when double-digit returns are available by gambling in currency speculation or derivatives. This diversion of capital away from socially-useful investment is one of the major forces fueling the 'casino economy'. That and the fact that investment opportunities in the goods-producing sector are shrinking due to the problem of 'over-capacity' – too many goods chasing too few buyers (see chapter 5). Computerized robots and automated assembly lines replace workers with new technology, leaving fewer people to actually buy products that factories are churning out. Those that remain find their wages under constant downward pressure in the face of cheaper labor elsewhere. The drive to be 'competitive' ends up being a race to the bottom. Workers who don't lose their jobs find their wages squeezed.

In Canada, which normally ranks near the top of UNDP's annual 'human development' rankings, a recent study found that the real disposable income on average fell by 3.3 per cent between 1989 and 1999. This coincided exactly with a period of neo-liberal economic policies including drastic cuts in government expenditures, reduced taxes and relatively high domestic interest rates.

'Families have had to work longer and longer hours in order to maintain the same level of earnings from employment and the idea of an affluent leisure society made possible by technological progress has become little more than a bad joke,' concluded a report published by the Canadian Center for Policy Alternatives.

Despite these worrying warning signs, staunch free marketers are reluctant to abandon their beliefs: 'Give the private sector the resources,' they say, 'and it will do the job.' But the proof is elusive. Surplus capital which doesn't get funneled into currency markets zips straight into overseas tax havens where both rich individuals and globe-trotting multinationals have been squirreling away their cash for decades.

There are nearly 70 tax havens scattered around the world. These 'offshore financial centers' include places like the Bahamas, the Cayman Islands, Liberia and Bermuda. Investors can store their wealth secretly, no questions asked – thus escaping any social obligations to the country where they may have earned it. Only a small number of these tax havens have public disclosure laws affecting the banks which operate within their borders.

The Economist estimates that the 1.2 per cent of the world population who live in tax havens produce about 3 per cent of the global GDP. Yet these countries account for 26 per cent of the world's financial assets and more than 30 per cent of the profits of US multinationals. This final figure gives a clear sense of how important tax havens are to the corporate world. But it also underlines the flawed reasoning of those who support economic policies premised on tax cuts and corporate deregulation. In almost all cases corporations will do whatever they can to avoid paying taxes. Private companies exist to maximize returns on the investment of their stockholders – they jeopardize their own survival to the extent that they are unable to reach that goal.

Enron example
This tension between the corporate world view and the broader public interest is one reason why tax havens are now coming under intense scrutiny. Countries

in the Organization of Economic Cooperation and Development (OECD) and in the EU have long recognized these havens as a drain on national treasuries and a convenient way of 'laundering' illegal funds. For example, the disgraced US energy trading company, Enron, is said to have used 800 different 'financial dumps' in the Caribbean to hide its debts. And it is estimated that up to $500 billion from the global narcotics trade passes through tax havens annually. There is now fear that the rise of electronic commerce combined with global financial liberalization will trigger an even greater flow of wealth and profits to these tax-free enclaves.[15]

While the number of super-wealthy expands, the social fabric, the backdrop to all our lives, continues to fray. This is the hidden human cost of 'market discipline' and it is as much a dilemma for European social democracies as it is for countries in Africa or Latin America.

All of us in the industrialized nations can chronicle the gradual decline in public services and social provision that has accompanied attempts to control government deficits. This cut-back on public spending is demanded by international markets, the same investors that demand higher rates of return on their investment and lower rates of taxation. As corporate profits boom and real wages stagnate, the glue that holds us together is losing its bond. As government revenues are steered to paying down debt or cutting taxes, we're told there is no longer enough money to pay for 'public goods'. Middle-class taxpayers, offered a few hundred dollars in cuts, in return receive deteriorating schools, reduced funding for parks and recreation facilities, inadequate public transport and a weakened healthcare system.

In Western Europe, Canada, Australia and New Zealand/Aotearoa public education and healthcare systems have seen repeated budget cuts as the state retreats and makes way for private, profit-oriented ventures. Welfare and unemployment benefits have been 'rationalized', slashing the number of those eligible. Senior citizens and those nearing retirement are fearful that promised pensions will evaporate as governments become more desperate for funds. Individuals are frantically scraping together whatever savings they have and heading towards the stock market in the hope that they too will ride to old-age security on the coattails of the FTSE, the NASDAQ and the Dow Jones. Government funding for the arts and for environmental protection has also been steadily eroded. This failure to protect these 'public goods' diminishes us all, makes us less capable of caring for each other and prohibits us from advancing together as a cohesive, mutually supportive community.

Globalization has also derailed development in the South where the poor continue to pay the highest price of adjustment. In order to boost exports and maintain their obligations to creditors, developing countries must divert money away from things like healthcare, education and aid to small-scale farmers. There have been countless studies detailing the social impact of economic globalization and the results are depressingly similar. The biggest impact is felt by the poor. In most of the world's poorest countries poverty reduction stalled from 1995-2005 as they fell further behind richer nations.

As Brazil's economy lurched into crisis in 1998 the IMF insisted on huge government cuts approaching a fifth of the budget. More than eight million of Brazil's poorest depend on subsidized rations of beans, rice and sugar for survival. The Government was forced to cut expenditure on those rations by more than half. At the same time the subsidy on school lunches was cut by 35 per cent. The 1999 budget for land reform, one of the most pressing social issues in Latin America, was reduced by 43 per cent.

Poverty, the environment and the market

Indian liberalization

The Indian Government launched its campaign to liberalize the economy and open up to foreign investors in 1992. In 15 years the giant nation has been transformed. Multinational brands are ubiquitous and sleek Japanese cars now jostle bullock carts in the streets of Mumbai and Hyderabad. High-tech exports are booming. In January 2006 Dell Inc., the world's biggest personal computer maker, announced it would open a fourth call centre in the country increasing its number of Indian employees to 15,000. Meanwhile, the country is graduating millions of skilled professionals and foreign capital is pouring in. Microsoft, Intel and Cisco all announced investments of a billion dollars or more in early 2006.[16]

Nonetheless opposition has been growing as disparities within the country grow. A 1997 Gallup poll found that two out of three Indians believed their standard of living had fallen or stagnated since embracing globalization. One in 11 Indian children dies before the age of five and malnutrition affects half the country's children. Ten per cent of all boys and a quarter of all girls don't attend primary school while the death rate for girls age 1-5 is 50 per cent greater than for boys.[13] Demonstrations have erupted across the country as farmers worry about cheap food imports wiping out local farmers. Two influential coalitions uniting hundreds of grassroots organizations are spearheading the protests. The National Alliance of Peoples' Movements is made up of more than 200 citizens' groups and was formed in 1993. The Joint Forum of Indian People Against Globalization (JAFIP) brought together more than 50 farmers' and peasant groups in 1998 to demand that India withdraw from the WTO.

The litany of suffering and damage spawned by harsh market reforms is repeated across the developing world. A massive study involving hundreds of civil-society groups across eight countries confirms this judgment.

The Structural Adjustment Participatory Review Initiative (SAPRI) held hearings from Bangladesh to El Salvador gathering grassroots information over a four-year period, originally with the participation of ex-World Bank President Jim Wolfensohn. However, when the Bank realized the outcome of the hearings it declined to participate in the release of the final report. No wonder. The SAPRI review confirmed what Northern NGOs and ordinary people in the South had been saying for years: 'Adjustment policies contributed to further impoverishment and marginalization of local populations while increasing economic inequality.'[17]

In Senegal, which had endured 20 years of IMF programs, the report found 'declining quality in education and health' combined with a growth in 'maternal mortality, unemployment and child labor'. In Tanzania, globalization had successfully redirected agriculture towards exports but had also 'expanded rural poverty, income inequality and environmental degradation'. Food security decreased, housing conditions deteriorated and primary-school enrolment dropped while malnutrition and infant mortality rose.

In Mexico, millions of farmers were pushed out of agriculture and thousands of small businesses went bankrupt. A decade after NAFTA, poverty, rural unemployment and overall inequality had all increased. In 1990, Mexico was self-sufficient in maize. Now it's the world's third largest importer. According to Carlos Ling, an Oxfam worker in Central America, after free trade poor Mexicans became dependent on 'bought seeds, on controlled and unequal markets and on powerful middlemen'.[18]

In Nicaragua, whose mildly leftist Sandinista government was destabilized by the US in the 1980s, IMF policies drove the country into further poverty. Financial deregulation attracted capital to 'short-term, high-interest deposits' and 'away from productive investment in small-scale domestic agriculture and manufacturing'. In Hungary, the IMF advised introducing liberalized trade, a tight money supply and rapid privatization of state assets. But the report found the policies deflected money away from education and social services and into the wallets of wealthy bond holders.

Poverty in Russia

But it was in Russia that the orthodox prescription for economic reform did some of its greatest harm. Supported by billions in Western aid, subsidized loans and rescheduled debt, the plan was to turn Russia into a capitalist success story overnight. Instead the 'shock therapy' threw the economy open to the winds of corruption. State assets were privatized, ending up in the hands of a small group of powerful insiders (often the same people who ran the former communist state apparatus) while ordinary Russians were saddled with colossal debts. At the same time an estimated $150 billion left the country, most of it permanently.

In the absence of price controls and with the loss of guaranteed employment, Russians endured poverty unknown for decades. From 1998-2000, more than 40 million Russians were forced below the poverty line. Today 25 per cent live below the poverty line and incomes are lower than they were in 1990. The country has experienced the steepest fall in peacetime living standards in modern history. According to the UN inequality doubled from 1989 to 1996. The income share of the richest 20 per cent of Russians was 11 times that of the poorest 20 per cent. Male life expectancy dropped from 70 years in the mid-1980s to 59 years in 2005. By 1996 the under-five child mortality rate was 25 per thousand live births – the same as Libya or Venezuela.[8]

In all countries touched by economic globalization, women tend to bear a disproportionate share of the costs. One feminist critique of structural adjustment documented many ways in which women become 'shock absorbers' for economic reforms. These include: forcing more women into 'informal' sector jobs as mainstream opportunities fade; promoting export crops which men tend to dominate; disrupting girls' education; increasing mortality rates and worsening female health; more domestic violence and stress; and an overall increase in the work load of women both inside and outside the home.[19]

Since women are the caregivers in most societies they tend to pick up the pieces when the social safety net is slashed. A 1997 Zimbabwe study found that 15 years of economic reform had a devastating impact on women in that southern African country. When school fees were raised, girls dropped out first and when health spending was cut by a third, the number of women dying in childbirth doubled. As male bread-winners are laid off, women do what they can to compensate for the lost income. They brew beer, turn to prostitution or become street traders. It inevitably falls on women to pick up the slack when governments cut education, healthcare and other social programs.[9]

Are the costs of growth too great? As the victims of globalization multiply, growing legions of ordinary people are beginning to question a process over which they have no control and little say. It's easy to be a cheerleader for economic globalization if you're on the winning side. But not so easy if your job has been outsourced to Mexico or China; or your coffee crop no longer brings in enough cash to feed and clothe your family. As the sinews of the global economy bind tighter, citizens, workers, students, women, small farmers and environmentalists have begun to speak out forcefully against a system which they see as both harmful and unjust.

Instead of a homogenized global culture shaped by the narrow demands of the 'money economy' there is a resurgent push for equity and sustainability. Instead of a deregulated globalization which rides roughshod over the rights of nation states and communities, civil society groups from Bolivia to China are calling for a radical restructuring. The aim is for an economic system more connected to real human needs and aspirations – and less geared to the anti-human machinations of the corporate-led free market. In the next chapter we'll look at how we might get there.

1 http://www.millenniumassessment.org/en/index.aspx. **2** 'China, India and the New World Order', C Flavin and G Gardner, *State of the World 2006* (WW Norton, New York, 2006). **3** *Our Ecological Footprint: reducing human impact on human health*, Mathis Wackernagel and William Rees (New Society Publishers, 1996). **4** Quoted in 'The global economy is a doomsday machine', Kalle Lasn, see www.adbusters.org/campaigns/economic-globaldoomsday.html. **5** 'Free market freefall', Gerald Greenfield, *Focus on the Global South*, www.focusweb.org/. **6** 'The price of cheap beef', George Monbiot, *The Guardian*, 18 October 2005. **7** 'Brazil's sick economy infects the ecosystem', Anthony Faiola, *Guardian Weekly*, 25 April 1999. **8** 'The end of the miracle', Walden Bello, *Multinational Monitor*, Jan/Feb 1998. **9** *The IMF: selling the environment short*, Friends of the Earth, see http://www.foe.org/res/pubs/pdf/imf.pdf. **10** 'Malagasy Wilderness in the Balance', Tim Cocks, BBC News, 14 February 2005, http://news.bbc.co.uk/2/hi/africa/4258781.stm. **11** *Globalization and its Discontents*, Joseph Stiglitz (WW Norton, New York, 2002). **12** *Human Development Report 1999* (UNDP, New York, 1999). **13** *Human Development Report 2005* (UNDP, New York, 2005). **14** 'Bush Policies Drive Surge in Corporate Tax Freeloading', see http://www.ctj.org/corpfed04pr.pdf. **15** 'No mean feat to crack down on tax havens', Madelaine Drohan, *The Globe and Mail*, Toronto, 12 April 2000. **16** 'Dell to add 5,000 employees in India', *Toronto Star*, 31 January 2006. **17** The policy roots of economic crisis and poverty', www.saprin.org/global_rpt.htm. **18** Oxfam Connections, 'Fair Trade vs Free Trade', September 2002, www.oxfam.org.au/publications/connections/september_2002/fairtradevsfreetrade.html. **18** 'Robbing Russia', *The Nation*, 4 October 1999. **19** *Mortgaging women's lives*, P Sparr (Zed Press, 1994).

7 Redesigning the global economy

Globalization is increasing inequality and poverty worldwide as national governments lose the ability to control their development strategies and policies. Political solutions are needed to reinvigorate democratic control both North and South. But political reforms need to be combined with structural reforms. In combination these should put meaningful employment and human rights at the heart of economic policy, boost local control and decision-making, and restore the ecological health and natural capital of our planet.

ECONOMIC GLOBALIZATION IS a powerful movement of people, goods, capital and ideas – driven by ideology, self-interest and bottom-line notions of economic efficiency.

But it is, essentially, an undemocratic process – one which is proceeding without the participation or knowledge of tens of millions of people who are most directly affected by the great economic upheavals of the last quarter century.

While it is true that globalization has boosted growth and lifted millions out of poverty over the past 15 years, the process has been, at best, uneven. And it has left inequality and environmental devastation in its wake. It has also been highly selective. Most of the gains have been in Asia, especially in China and India. New investment in those countries has reduced the numbers of extreme poor by half-a-billion people since 1990. The Chinese economy has been on a tear. In 2005, the country used more than a quarter of the world's steel and nearly half its cement. China is also the largest oil consumer after the US, and the world's biggest producer and consumer of coal. Within 20-30 years its economy will outstrip that of the United States. The Chinese auto industry is just beginning to spread its wings and established car manufacturers are cowering in anticipation. The Chinese firms Geely, Chery Automobile and Lifan Group are poised to flood world markets with cheap, fuel-efficient cars.

Unfortunately, globalization in these two countries has come with a huge cost: poisoned rivers, deadly air, depleted soils, the world's worst acid rain, and the largest migration from the countryside to the urban areas in history.

According to the Worldwatch Institute: 'Land degradation, depleting aquifers, water pollution and urban claims on land and water are nibbling away at China and India's agricultural foundations – and may soon make it impossible for them to meet their rapidly expanding food needs.'[1]

Rapid growth has also heightened regional disparities and increased the gap between rich and poor. On average workers in Indian cities earn nearly 40 per cent more than those in the countryside. In China, wage gaps are greatest between the booming eastern cities and poorer rural areas. Annual incomes in Beijing and Shanghai average more than $1,000 while rural incomes are closer to $370. China still has 600 million citizens living on less than $2 a day and India has another 800 million people in the same boat. Fearing social unrest as inequality grows President Hu Jintao has admitted that China needs to build a 'more balanced and harmonious society'.

Meanwhile, globalization has completely ignored other parts of the world. In sub-Saharan Africa, between 1990 and 2002, per-capita income didn't rise at all. The number of people living on less than a dollar a day increased by a third, to more than 330 million. As UNDP notes, income inequality is increasing in countries that account for more than 80 per cent of the world's population.[2]

The overwhelming conclusion is that economic globalization has tragically failed the world's poor. As it is impoverishing millions of our fellow humans it is radically altering social relationships, stripping age-old cultures of their identity and threatening the environmental health of the Earth.

There is no doubt that globalization is powerful and that the forces behind it are formidable. But an exclusionary, top-down, unequal form of globalization is not inevitable. For the simple reason that the economic structures which shape the global systems of production and distribution are human-made. The institutions which make the rules which govern the operation of the world economy are human-made. And the governments that we elect are people like us who choose to represent the interests of all citizens, at least in theory. Change is possible. Indeed, change is inevitable.

The crisis of globalization is a unique opportunity for addressing core issues of democracy and human development. It has invigorated a worldwide peoples' movement whose loud demands for change are attracting more and more attention and support: from consumers, environmentalists, trade unionists, women, religious activists, farmers, human rights advocates and ordinary citizens.

The World Social Forum is one of the most visible expressions of opposition – an annual gathering of thousands of such groups from around the globe. The WSF was born in the aftermath of massive demonstrations against the World Trade Organization in Seattle in November 1999. It was initially organized to coincide with the annual gathering of political and business leaders at the World Economic Forum in Davos, Switzerland. The first three WSF meetings were held in Porto Alegre, Brazil. The fourth forum in Mumbai in 2004 drew more than 100,000 people. The 2006 forum was held in three different centers – Caracas, Karachi and Bamako, Mali – to encourage more regional collaboration. Activists from more than 150 countries have attended these huge events but the WSF has also spawned dozens of local, regional and national social forums. These face-to-face encounters provide citizens' groups a chance to compare notes, to strategize and to hammer out alternatives to the prevailing model of economic globalization. This is not an anti-globalization movement as much as it is a pro-peoples movement. The motto of the WSF is 'another world is possible'. It is in essence a network of networks focusing on global issues of social and economic justice, interacting when necessary but mostly working independently on their own issues in their own countries or communities.

Social Forum movement

The Social Forum movement has so far managed to avoid fracturing into sectarianism and has avoided alliance with specific political parties – to its credit. As the saying goes, 'politics is the art of compromise'. The WSF understands that in order to influence change the movement needs to remain independent of formal politics, acting both as a conscience and a goad. And there is good reason for this. Even the most socially progressive political leaders can be forced into tight corners by the powerful gatekeepers of the global economic system. Yesterday's hero, bravely confronting the IMF or the WTO, can quickly become tomorrow's victim of the 'Washington Consensus'.

Other campaigns to rein in the globalization juggernaut have succeeded in educating millions about global inequalities. The Jubilee 2000 campaign to cancel Third World debt galvanized hundreds of thousands of supporters, both north and south. More recently the Make Poverty History movement and the global Trade Justice Campaign have continued to push for significant changes to the world trading system to improve the lives of millions of the world's poor.

Speaking on behalf of the Trade Justice Campaign before the December 2005 WTO meeting in Hong Kong, Nelson Mandela said: 'There is a chance to make decisions that will lift billions of people out of poverty. Trade can be part of the solution to poverty but at the moment it's part of the problem.'

The global campaign for trade justice continues in the wake of the failed Hong Kong talks where industrialized nations continued to drag their feet on the relaxation of agricultural subsidies for Southern exports. The rich nations pushed through 'plurilateral' negotiations on services, what one critic called an attempt to 'corral many developing countries into sectoral negotiations designed to blast open key services'.

According to Focus on the Global South Director, Walden Bello, the South was promised a final phase-out date for Northern agricultural export subsidies which is little more than window dressing. 'Even with the phase-out of formally defined export subsidies, he writes, 'other forms of export support will allow the European Union to continue to subsidize exports to the tune of 55 billion euros after 2013.'[3]

Political leaders are feeling increased pressure to act on behalf of the world's poorest people.

Across Latin America opposition to globalization has exploded since Brazil's 1998 economic crisis and the collapse of the Argentinean economy in 2002 – both of which were caused by hard-line IMF policies and meddling by financial speculators. Following the election of former labor activist Ignacio 'Lula' da Silva in Brazil, leaders opposed to market fundamentalism have been elected in Argentina, Venezuela, Bolivia, Uruguay and Chile. At the November 2005 Summit of the Americas in Buenos Aires, those nations spearheaded opposition to the proposed Free Trade Area of the Americas (FTAA), derailing plans to extend free trade from the Arctic to Patagonia. The five dissenting nations rejected the US-led plan claiming in the summit's closing declaration that 'conditions do not exist to attain a hemispheric free-trade accord that is balanced and fair with access to markets and free of subsidies and distorted commercial practices.'

Those who control the global economy are taking note. As far back as 1999, at the Asia Pacific Economic Cooperation (APEC) meetings in New Zealand, then-US trade negotiator Charlene Barshefsky hinted that the single greatest threat to globalization is 'the absence of public support'. Her concerns are justified. There is now a worldwide citizens' movement to rethink the global economy from the ground up. It is a movement which is becoming stronger by the day. And it is premised on one shared and unshakeable central truth. The only way to convince states to act in the interests of their people is to construct a system that will put humans back in control at the center of economic activity. This is an enormous project but one in which millions of people in scores of countries around the globe are actively engaged. What follows are a few of the ideas for change currently being debated.

Changing the system
1 Revamp the IMF
Some critics suggest abolishing the IMF; others support a radical transformation. But both sides are agreed that the IMF, the WTO and the World Bank need to become more democratic and more focused on the needs and interests of the citizens of the world rather than fixated on narrow goals of market fundamentalism.

The IMF has been around for more than half a century. In all that time it has still not learned to put people ahead of markets. Change is long overdue.

In the short term both the Bank and the Fund need to be more accountable, more democratic and more transparent in their decision-making. A fairer voice to developing countries would be a big first step.

The Fund must also be made more accountable to its members. In the past it has been arrogant and closed to criticism or suggestion. In its operations overseas, the Fund should consult with social and environmental ministries, parliament and civil society organizations in addition to the ministries of finance. To improve its accountability, it should be subject to regular external evaluations of its programs and policies.

The IMF must end its love affair with conditionality – Fund-speak for the political and economic conditions attached to its loans. A largely unaccountable body like the IMF should not be telling elected governments how to do their job.

Fund staff have to move beyond their current comfortable circuit of Finance Ministry officials to talk (and listen) to trade unions, peasant organizations, women's groups and non-governmental organizations – the people who will be on the receiving end of the social impact of any agreement. It should have to convince governments that it is right, rather than coerce them into adopting policies with which they disagree.

The Fund must make improving the lives of ordinary people central to its policies. This may seem obvious. But in practice its staff often behave as if people were at the service of markets, not the other way round. That still leaves the IMF with an important role in promoting economic stability and low inflation. Boom-bust cycles and escalating prices hurt the poor more than anyone.

Perhaps more important is the need for a complete change in the organizational culture of the Fund. It must become open to the public, not closed; pluralist and open-minded, not dogmatic. It must listen, not lecture; and it must learn from its mistakes.

A dogmatic, deregulating Fund will merely exacerbate the chronic instability and inequality of the global market. A Fund with a renewed moral purpose and democratic mandate could bring those same forces of chaos under control, to the benefit of the majority of the world's citizens.

Adapted from 'Dogmatists in dark suits', Duncan Green,
New Internationalist, No 320, Jan/Feb 2000.

2 Support a tax on financial speculation

Unregulated investment has turned the global economy into a casino where speculators search for instant profits, ignoring the human consequences of their actions. Currency markets perform a useful function. It's a way of taking the worry out of international buying-and-selling by figuring out today what a future purchase will cost. But it's estimated only 2-4 per cent of currency trading has to do with real market exchanges. The rest is pure speculation, making money off money. A tax on financial speculation that would put people ahead of profits is urgently needed. Such a tax could help stabilize global markets and capture much-needed funds for global development.

There is a significant movement to support such a tax. In 1978 the Nobel Prize-winning economist James Tobin proposed that a small worldwide tariff (less than half of one per cent) be levied by all major countries on foreign-exchange transactions in order to 'throw some sand in the wheels' of speculative flows. Now the global justice movement, led by Attac in France (Association pour la Taxation des Transactions pour l'Aide aux Citoyens) is advocating a two-tier tax on financial transactions developed by the German economist, Bernd Spahn. The tax is designed to dampen speculation and to raise funds to support global development – a rare opportunity to capture the enormous wealth of an untaxed sector and redirect it towards the public good. Most of the time the tax would be levied at a very low rate, around a tenth of a per cent. But in times of crisis the second tier would kick in at a much higher rate.

The main barrier to the Spahn tax is not technical, it's political. The tax is seen as a threat by the financial community and has met with stiff resistance by a sector with massive political clout. The very idea of putting people ahead of markets challenges the foundations of the current global economic model and those who control it.

Adapted from 'Time for Tobin', Robin Round, *New Internationalist*, No 320, Jan/Feb 2000 with information from Attac, http://www.france.attac.org/

3 Control capital for the public good

Capital needs to be seen primarily as an instrument or means of development not as a tool for turning a quick profit at the expense of people and the Earth. New global investment rules at the World Trade Organization and the North American Free Trade Agreement (NAFTA) give carte blanche to wealthy investors while demanding nothing in return. An alternative investment code is needed for democratic control of capital and to stimulate investment that benefits local communities. Such a code would include citizens' rights, government responsibilities and corporate obligations based on these key elements:

Fair treatment – Foreign investment would be welcome provided social obligations were met. The concept of 'national treatment', which is used to force governments to treat foreign corporations on the same terms as domestic companies, should be discarded. Instead the 'stored value' of capital would be the basis for establishing obligations for fair treatment of foreign-based corporations.

Social obligations – Governments would have the legal right to require all corporations, both foreign and domestic, to meet basic social obligations such as labor standards, environmental safeguards and social-security contributions.

Performance standards – To ensure that foreign investment serves national-development priorities, governments would be allowed to require standards such as job quotas, balancing imports with exports, quotas on natural-resource exports or restrictions on the repatriation of profits.

Investment incentives – To ensure that corporations

keep these social obligations, governments may use investment 'incentives' including: grants, loans and subsidies; procurement practices; tax incentives and limits on profit remittances for foreign companies that fail their social obligations.

Public enterprises – All governments have a responsibility to use tax revenues for protecting the 'commons' through public investments. These could include exercising public ownership over key sectors of the economy; establishing social programs and public services; safeguarding ecologically sensitive areas; and protecting cultural heritage.

Expropriation measures – A foreign corporation could not demand compensation for an environmental law that placed a quota on the export of a nonrenewable resource or a health ban on the sale of toxic substances, on the grounds that such measures would reduce the corporation's profit margins. Nor could a foreign company claim compensation for loss of future profits because government actions prevent a planned investment from going ahead.

Financial transactions – All governments have a right to require that foreign investment be used for productive rather than speculative purposes.

Dispute settlement – In the event of a dispute, citizens, governments and corporations would all have the right to be heard. To ensure that non-governmental organizations, native communities, environment and women's groups, trade unions and others have equal access to the dispute-settlement mechanism, national and international funds should be established for citizen interveners.

Adapted from 'Rewriting the rules', Tony Clarke, *New Internationalist*, No 320, Jan/Feb 2000.

4 Support fair trade

In 1988 'Max Havelaar', the first fair trade certification initiative, was launched in Holland. The name was taken from a fictional character who opposed the exploitation of coffee pickers in Dutch colonies. In 1997, the Fair Trade Labeling Organization (FLO) brought Max Havelaar together with counterparts in other countries. Today, the FLO operates in 19 countries in Europe, Japan, North America, Mexico, Australia and New Zealand.

Compared to conventional trading structures, these Alternative Trade Organizations offer higher returns to producers in the developing world through direct trade and fair prices. The fair trade movement is a response to a global trading system that is both unjust and exploitative – global trading rules are rigged to benefit the rich and marginalize the poor. Fixing the global system will take major institutional changes and a determined campaign.

Unregulated trade allows corporations to pit workers against each another, to reduce the bargaining strength of trade unions, to strip away benefits, to ignore dangerous working conditions and to reduce wages.

Instead, trade agreements must bolster the rights of working people by promoting labor rights – including the freedom to form trade unions and bargain collectively. Free trade is a social issue as well as an economic one. To attract investors, countries compete to lower costs. That can trigger a 'race to the bottom' where job hungry nations offer cheap labor, weak environmental laws, lax health and safety standards or reduced social services. Governments must have the right to regulate foreign investment to protect their citizens and to link investment to national development priorities.

Nations should have the power to establish and defend intellectual property rules that protect the interests of their citizens. Trade agreements must guarantee access to essential drugs, prohibit the erosion of traditional cultures and protect indigenous knowledge and biodiversity.

Redesigning the global economy

If democracy is to have meaning, citizens must help formulate trade rules. These agreements must promote civil and political rights as well as the social, cultural, economic and environmental rights of peoples and communities.

In the meantime the fair trade movement provides a chance to find out about the blatant unfairness of the global trading system. And to set standards that could redefine global trade to include social and environmental considerations.

Fair trade principles

- Producers are paid a fair price and workers a fair wage. For crops like coffee, tea and bananas, farmers are paid a stable minimum price. The links between buyers and sellers are shortened, doing away with 'middle men'.
- Buyers and producers develop long-term relationships of mutual support and benefit.
- All aspects of the trading relationship are open to public accountability.
- Exploitative child labor and forced labor are prohibited. Working conditions are healthy and safe.
- Goods are produced and crops grown in an environmentally sustainable way.

---

1 *State of the World 2006*, Worldwatch Institute, (WW Norton, New York, 2006). **2** *Human Development Report 2005* (UNDP, New York, 2005). **3** 'The Real Meaning of Hong Kong: Brazil and India Join the Big Boys' Club', Walden Bello, www.focusweb.org, 22 December 2005.

Contacts

International
Focus on the Global South, www.focusweb.org
International Forum on Globalization, www.ifg.org
Third World Network, www.twnside.org
ATTAC (Association for the taxation of financial transactions for the aid of citizens), www.attac.org
World Social Forum, www.forumsocialmundial.org.br
ActionAid, www.actionaid.org
Transnational Institute, www.tni.org

Aotearoa/New Zealand
Arena, www.arena.org.nz

Australia
Aftinet (Australian Fair Trade and Investment Network), www.aftinet.org.au

Canada
Canadian Centre for Policy Alternatives, www.policyalternatives.ca
Council of Canadians, www.canadians.org
Halifax Initiative, www.halifaxinitiative.org
Polaris Institute, www.polarisinstitute.org

UK
War on want, www.waronwant.org
ActionAid, www.actionaid.org.uk
Oxfam, www.oxfam.org.uk
World Development Movement, www.wdm.org.uk

USA
Institute for Food and Development Policy (Food First) www.foodfirst.org
Institute of Policy Studies, www.ips-dc.org
Public Citizen/Global Trade Watch, www.citizen.org/trade
Global Exchange, www.globalexchange.org

Bibliography

Another world is possible if..., Susan George, Verso, London, 2004.

Dilemmas of domination: the unmaking of the American Empire, Walden Bello, Metropolitan Books, Henry Holt and Company, New York, 2005.

False Dawn: the delusions of global capitalism, John Gray (Granta Books, London, 1998)

Free trade for all: how trade can promote development, Joseph Stiglitz and Andrew Charlton, Oxford University Press, Oxford/New York, 2006.

Globalization and its discontents, Joseph Stiglitz, WW Norton, New York, 2003.

For the Common Good, Herman E Daly and John B Cobb Jr, (Beacon Press, Boston, 1989)

Human Development Report 2005, United Nations Development Programme, New York, 2005.

Jihad vs McWorld, Benjamin R Barber (Ballantine Books, New York, 1995)

State of the World 2006, Worldwatch Institute, WW Norton, NewYork/London, 2006.

The Cancer Stage of Capitalism, John McMurtry (Pluto Press, London, 1999)

The Crisis of Global Capitalism, George Soros (Perseus Books, 1998)

The Post-Corporate World: life after capitalism, David Korten (Kumarian and Berrett-Koehler, San Francisco, CA and West Hartford, CT 1999)

Your money or your life: the tyranny of global finance, Eric Toussaint, Haymarket Books, Chicago, 2006.

New Internationalist, **www.newint.org**

Index

Index

Index

Index

P. 85 - ₱.
P. 87 - end of 2nd ₱ - issue of immediate gain - fostered by a near-sighted interest
p. 89 - 2nd ₱ -> 'enticing' foreign investors -> control?
p. 90
p. 95 - 3rd ₱. Catch 22